How to Sound Clever

**Master the 600 everyday words you
pretend to understand...when you don't**

Hubert van den Bergh

Illustrations by www.sandrahowgate.com

A & C Black • London

First published in Great Britain 2010

A & C Black Publishers Ltd
36 Soho Square, London W1D 3QY
www.acblack.com

A CIP record for this book is available from the British Library.

ISBN: 9-781-4081-2509-0

This book is produced using paper that is made from wood grown in managed, sustainable forests. It is natural, renewable and recyclable. The logging and manufacturing processes conform to the environmental regulations of the country of origin.

Design by Fiona Pike, Pike Design, Winchester
Typeset by Saxon Graphics Ltd, Derby
Printed and bound in Great Britain by MPG Books Limited

Introduction

A couple of years ago, I was in a meeting trying to persuade some people of the merits of a business idea. The presentation seemed to be going well: the three people opposite me were nodding as I spoke. After ten minutes I stopped talking and put my pen down on the table in what I hoped was a business-deal-sealing kind of way. Then one of them spoke. 'You kept on using the word *salubrious*,' he said. 'Do you know what the word actually means?'

I should confess at this point that *salubrious* is one of those words I've never been sure about. It sounds like the French word for *dirty*, which is *sale*, but I can never remember if it in fact means the opposite: if it means *clean*. I had to go for one or the other now.

'Er...doesn't it mean *dirty*?,' I said weakly.

He shook his head. '*Salubrious* means the opposite – it means *clean*.'

The deal collapsed five minutes later.

Now, that particular gentleman may have been a stickler, but his point stands: if you can't be trusted with your use of those most elementary units of communication, words, then what can you be trusted with exactly?

That incident was the catalyst for this book. Over a two-year period, I looked up every word I didn't understand when I heard it in a conversation or read it in a newspaper. But is this book for you? Have a look at the three sentences below – if you don't understand the

How to Sound Clever

words in bold, then you'll get something of out this book. Be honest; don't **dissimulate** (turn to p. 51 if you're not sure of this word):

> Manchester United's shirt sales depend on the club's continued **hegemony** (p. 90)
>
> A **phalanx** (p. 150) of security guards monitors Obama
>
> Journalists often describe stock markets as **febrile** (p. 70)

The three words highlighted above are part of a group that we all struggle with – these are the words we find **abstruse** (p. 5) yet nod to during conversations; the words that we see in newspaper articles and hope their context will **elucidate** (p. 60).

But the problem with leading our lives in this way is this:

> *If we need a word's context to understand its meaning, it follows that we lack the confidence to use that word ourselves.*

Which means that, after our **halcyon** (p. 87) schooldays are over, our vocabulary never improves.

This book contains 600 or so English words that we're always meaning to look up. Each word summons up a concept that is **idiosyncratic** (p. 96); and so each word increases your ability to express what is in your head. And the unintended **corollary** (p. 39) of your using language in this more precise way is that you will sound clever.

For each word, I list its root and then give an example of how to use it, such as:

perfunctory (adj.)
= *(of an action)* **done carelessly, as a matter of routine**
from the Latin *perfunctorius*: careless

e.g. *Breakfast at Tiffany's* author Truman Capote hated writing, so postponed it by sharpening pencils for hours: he found this **perfunctory** action soothing

The place for this book is on top of your bedside table or toilet cistern. Once you've flicked through it as you nod off or focus on **scatological** (p. 181) matters, you'll start to notice these 600 words everywhere. It's like buying a new car, a BMW, say; in the weeks afterwards, BMWs

seem to fill the roads – not because their number has **proliferated** (p. 160) but because you are more alert to their presence.

Soon you will be so comfortable with these 600 words that you can use them yourself. This will give you a kick because you are expressing yourself in as **pellucid** (p. 147) a fashion as possible; and the unintended consequence of this is that your sentences will become **lapidary** (p. 110) and, as it happens, you will sound clever. So, enjoy...

This book is dedicated to my mother, with her gift for science; and for my father, with his gift for art.

A

abstruse (adj.)
= **hard to understand** from the Latin *abstrudere*: to conceal

e.g. When we can recall events from our dreams, they seem **abstruse** to us

actuate (verb)
= **to put into motion** from the medieval Latin *actuare*: to carry out

e.g. When you leave the house, you must tap in a pin code to **actuate** the alarm

acuity (noun)
= **sharpness of mind or of the senses** from the Latin *acuere*: to sharpen

e.g. The oratory of Barack Obama's speeches reflects his intellectual **acuity**

adage / aphorism (noun)
= **a proverb expressing a universal truth** *adage derives from the Latin* adagium: *a saying (based on an early form of* aio: *I say);* aphorism *from the Greek* aphorismos: *a definition*

e.g. One of Oscar Wilde's best-known **aphorisms / adages** is: 'a little sincerity is a dangerous thing, and a great deal of it is absolutely fatal'

adduce (verb)
= **to cite by way of evidence** from the Latin *adducere*, from *ad-*: toward, and *ducere*: to lead

e.g. Mark Twain passed on investing in Alexander Bell's telephone, wrongly **adducing** that static on the line would mean no one would buy the device

adjunct (noun)
= **a thing added to something else but as a non-core part** from the Latin *ad-*: to, and *jungere*: to join

e.g. Women find that more attention from men is an **adjunct** to breast augmentation

adjutant (noun)
= **a deputy** from the Latin *adjuvare*: to assist

e.g. To show he was serious about his government being a coalition, Conservative David Cameron appointed Liberal Democrat Nick Clegg as his **adjutant**

aegis (noun)
= **the protection of a particular body** *for etymology, see box below*

e.g. George Bush Snr was forced to punish Saddam for attacking Kuwait because Kuwait is under the **aegis** of the US

According to The Iliad *(the Greek poem written by Homer in the 8th century BC), the **aegis** (or* aigis *in Greek) was the shield wielded by Zeus, the king of the gods. From the shield hung one hundred golden tassels, which were depicted by Classical vase-painters as writhing snakes.*

*Today, we continue to use the word **aegis** to denote any protection afforded to one person by another and it is often used to describe one country's looking after another in the international arena.*

---

agent provocateur (noun)
= **a person who seeks to harm another by provoking them to commit an unlawful or wrong act** from the French *agent provocateur*: inciting agent

e.g. In the film *Donnie Brasco*, Johnny Depp plays an FBI agent who infiltrates the Mafia and encourages their criminality; Depp is an **agent provocateur**

---

alabaster (adj.)
= **smooth and white** from the Latin *alabaster*: a perfume casket made from the mineral alabaster; *alabaster literally means 'resembling alabaster, a white variety of gypsum'*

e.g. Nicole Kidman's ginger locks contrast with her **alabaster** skin

aleatory (adj.)
= **random** from the Latin *alea*: a game with dice (singular of 'die'); *aleatory literally means 'depending on the toss of a die'*

e.g. Travelling across London at the weekend can be a somewhat **aleatory** experience in view of the improvement works on the underground

amanuensis (noun)
= **an assistant to an artist** from the Latin *(servus) a manu*: (slave) at hand(writing), and -*ensis*: belonging to

e.g. Agatha Christie had difficulty with writing and spelling owing to a learning disability so dictated all her detective stories to an **amanuensis**

amulet (noun)
= **a small piece of jewellery thought to ward off evil** *for etymology, see box below*

e.g. After breaking up with his fiancée, James Dean wore an enamel locket containing strands of her hair: this was his lucky **amulet**

---

amulet derives from the Latin amuletum, *meaning an object that protects a person from trouble.*

Examples of amulets include gems, rings and coins; all these objects are small enough to carry around and are believed to bring good luck to the bearer.

Amulets also exist in larger form and perhaps the most famous amulet is the crucifix, which is found in the homes of Christians to protect against evil.

anachronistic (adj.)
= **very old-fashioned** from the Greek *anakhronismos*, from *ana-*: backward, and *khronos*: time; *anachronistic literally means appropriate to a different time*

e.g. The Tower of London is guarded by Beefeaters who dress **anachronistically**

anaemic (adj.)
= **lacking in vigour** from the Greek *anaemia*, from *an-*: without, and *haima*: blood; *anaemic literally means 'suffering from anaemia'; this is a medical condition caused by a deficiency of red blood cells, resulting in paleness and weakness*

e.g. Compared with Rita Hayworth and other voluptuous stars of her day, Grace Kelly appeared **anaemic**

anodyne (adj.)
= **not contentious, often deliberately so** from the Greek *anodunos*: painless, from *an-*: without, and *odune*: pain

e.g. *The Great Gatsby* author F. Scott Fitzgerald didn't believe in **anodyne** entrances, once turning up to a Hollywood party on all fours and barking

anomic (adj.)
= *(of a person)* **lacking normal ethical standards** from the
Greek *anomos*: lawless

e.g. Serial killer Fred West murdered people on a whim:
he was an **anomic** individual

antediluvian (adj.)
= **so old-fashioned as to be ridiculous**
from the Latin *ante-*: before, and *diluvium*: flood;
*antediluvian literally means 'from a time before the flood
created by God to punish man' (as described in the Bible)*

e.g. Critics of the Catholic Church view the refusal to
ordain women as **antediluvian**

anthropogenic (adj.)
= *(usually of environmental pollutants)* **created by humans**
from the Greek *anthropos*: human being and *genic*:
produced by

e.g. The ozone is shrinking due to **anthropogenic** carbon
dioxide emissions

anthropomorphise (verb)
= **to attribute human form to something not human, such as an animal** from the Greek *anthropos*: human being, and *morphe*: form

e.g. Humans like watching dogs open doors with their paws – as though they had hands – because we like to **anthropomorphise** animals

apocryphal (adj.)
= *(of a story)* **of dubious authenticity, but relayed as if true (and having the ring of truth)** *for etymology, see box below*

e.g. Although it is true that he declared himself Emperor, the story that Napoleon performed the coronation himself is **apocryphal** - this duty went to Pope Pius VII

apocryphal derives from the Greek noun Apocrypha, *which means 'having been hidden away'. The early Christian Church gave this label to religious writings considered useful but not inspired by God - hence these volumes were excluded from the accepted canon of scripture.*

*Today, when we label a story **apocryphal**, it means we are casting doubt on its authenticity.*

apologist (noun)
= **a person who defends a cause that people find controversial** from the Greek *apologizesthai*: to give an account

e.g. Apologists for Nazism are treated with contempt by most people

apostatise (verb)
= **to abandon a religious or political belief** from the Greek *apostates*: a runaway slave

e.g. In some interpretations of sharia law, Muslims who have **apostatised** deserve death

apparatchik (noun)
= *(derogatory in tone)* **an official in a huge organisation**
from the Russian, *apparat*: apparatus, and *-chik*: denoting
agent

e.g. Within the Conservative Party, George Osborne is no
mere **apparatchik**, for he is one of David Cameron's
closest advisers and the Chancellor

apposite (adj.)
= **appropriate** from the Latin *appositus*, past participle of
apponere: to apply (from *ad-*: toward, and *ponere*: to put)

e.g. It is **apposite** to wear black to a funeral

approbation (noun)
= **approval** from the Latin *approbare*: to approve

e.g. Bill Gates' donation of billions to charity was greeted
with global **approbation**

Arcadian (noun)
= **relating to a paradise in the country** *for etymology, see
box below*

e.g. Many town-dwellers dream of leading **Arcadian**
existence

---

*Arcadia is in Greek mythology the home of Pan, the god
of flocks and herds; hence today the use of the word
Arcadia to signify a rural paradise.*

*(Incidentally, the god Pan gives us another word derived
from his name: **panic**. This is because the Greeks
represented Pan as being frightening in appearance –
having the horns and legs of a goat but a man's body –
which caused anyone who saw him to panic.)*

---

arcane (adj.)
= **shut off to outsiders, hence mysterious** from the Latin *arca*: a chest, from *arcere*: to shut up

e.g. To a Christian, the customs of a Muslim wedding ceremony – such as the elaborate decorating of the bride's hands and feet with henna seems **arcane**

archipelago (noun)
= **islands grouped together; OR a sea containing islands grouped together** from the Greek *arkhi-*: chief, and *pelagos*: sea

e.g. The West Indies form an **archipelago** lying between the Caribbean Sea and the Atlantic Ocean

argot (noun)
= **the slang of a particular clique** (*usually one under threat from society, such as criminals*) from the French *argot*: slang

e.g. The police are called 'the pigs' in the **argot** of criminals

arriviste (noun)
= **an ambitious person who has only recently 'made it'** from the French *arriver*: to arrive

e.g. People who have inherited wealth regard people whose wealth derives from their own endeavours as **arrivistes**

assiduous (adj.)
= **very diligent** from the Latin *assidere*: to be engaged in doing

e.g. Conspiracy theorists say the disappearance of the phone records for Marilyn Monroe's flat on the night of her death is evidence of an **assiduous** cover-up

atavistic (adj.)
= **concerning the re-emergence of traits that had disappeared generations ago** from the Latin *atavus*: forefather

e.g. A human foetus starts life with a tail; but as the foetus grows this **atavistic** feature drops off

attrition (noun)
= **the process of slowly reducing the strength of someone or something by pressure over time** from the Latin *atterere*: to rub

e.g. By continually returning the ball, Rafael Nadal wears out his opponents by a process of **attrition**

Augean (adj.)
= *(of a challenge)* **needing so much effort to finish as to seem impossible** *for etymology, see box below*

e.g. After overthrowing Saddam Hussein, President Bush faced the **Augean** task of establishing a democracy in Iraq

---

Augean derives from the name of King Augeas, who was best known in Greek mythology for his stables, which held the biggest herd of cattle in the country.

These cattle were so strong and healthy – in fact divinely so – that they produced huge heaps of dung every day, meaning that no one could ever clean out the stables properly.

*One of Hercules's 12 labours was to make these stables clean in just 24 hours; he succeeded in this by diverting the path of two rivers into the buildings, thus sweeping away the excrement. Today we continue to refer to any task that seems impossible as **Augean**.*

(auspices) under the auspices of (phrase)
= **with the protection of** *for etymology, see box below*

e.g. When Russia invaded Georgia, the UN objected because Georgia falls **under the auspices of** the UN

---

*The expression **under the auspices of** derives from the Latin auspicium, which means an observation by a soothsayer who relied on the flight of birds to divine the future.* Auspicium *itself derives from the Latin words* avis: *a bird, and* specere: *to observe.*

*If the soothsayer liked what he saw in the sky – in other words, if the **auspicium**, or birdwatching, was favourable – he would tell his client that the gods approved a particular plan. Hence, today, the expression **under the auspices of** someone means 'with the protection of' someone.*

---

autocrat (noun)
= **someone who demands total obedience from other people** from the Greek *autokrates*, from *autos-*: self, and *kratos*: power; *an **autocrat** literally means 'a ruler who has absolute power'*

e.g. Idi Amin was an autocrat who ruled Uganda with an iron rod, tolerating no dissent

autodidact (noun)
= **a self-taught person** from the Greek *autodidaktos*: self-taught, from *autos-*: self, and *didaktos*: taught

e.g. He left school with no qualifications, became an **autodidact** and now lectures the world over an Italian art

automaton (noun)
= **a person who seems to behave in a way that is more mechanical than human** from the Greek *automatos*: acting of itself, from *autos-*: self, and *matos*: willing

e.g. Author Virginia Woolf drowned herself by putting stones into her pockets and walking calmly into a river like an **automaton**

bacchanalian (adj.)
= **characterised by drunkenness and partying** *for etymology, see box overleaf*

e.g. After success in Hollywood, Marilyn Monroe developed an addiction to pills and *Dom Perignon*: hers was a **bacchanalian** lifestyle

bacchanalian originates from the name of Bacchus, a Roman god.

Bacchus was at first the god of fertility in nature and was thus at the centre of wild religious ceremonies; later Bacchus continued this association with abandonment by being known as the god of wine who reduced inhibitions and promoted creativity in the arts.

(Bacchus was the name given by the Romans to the Greek God Dionysus, see Dionysian)

badinage (noun)
= **witty talk** from the French *badiner*: to joke

e.g. The Queen Mother used to enjoy a nightly gin and tonic along with some **badinage**

bathetic (adj.)
= **relating to an anticlimax** (the kind that occurs when the mood unintentionally lurches from awe to ridicule) from the Greek *bathos*: depth

e.g. 'Does nobody understand?' were the final words of novelist James Joyce: a **bathetic** last statement for such a master of communication

beetle-browed (adj.)
= *(of a person's eyebrows)* **shaggy and projecting** from the Old English *beetle*, and *brow*, which meant 'eyebrow' (not 'forehead' as it does today)

e.g. Old men who do not trim their eyebrows become **beetle-browed**

behemoth (noun)
= **a huge thing, especially an enormous organisation**
from the Hebrew, *behemah*: beast

e.g. Jonathan Ross was one of the highest-paid employees of the **behemoth** that is the BBC

bellicose (adj.)
= **eager to fight** from the Latin *bellicus*: pertaining to war

e.g. Genghis Khan's **bellicose** nature led to conquests that created one of the largest empires in history

benighted (adj.)
= **ignorant due to a lack of education** from the 16th-century English *benight*: cover in darkness

e.g. The credit crunch began when onerous mortgages issued to financially **benighted** families in America went unpaid

bifurcate (verb)
= **to split up into two branches** from the Latin *bifurcus*: two-forked, from *bi-*: two, and *furca*: fork

e.g. By day Dr Jekyll was a model citizen but at night he turned into the monstrous Mr Hyde: the man led a **bifurcated** life

bilious (adj.)
= **full of spite** *for etymology, see box below*

e.g. Rock Hudson's agent arranged for the star to marry his secretary so that the press would not direct **bilious** comments towards Rock about his homosexuality

---

bilious derives from the Latin bilis, *meaning 'bile', which is a bitter fluid emitted by the liver to aid digestion; the ancient Greeks believed that bile had a negative influence on someone's mood (hence our use of the word* **bilious** *today to signify a bad-tempered person).*

Note that the word **bilious** *has the following extra meanings:*

- *(of a person) feeling sick*
  e.g. I felt **bilious** *after eating a dodgy egg*
- *(of a colour) so vivid as to be sickly*
  e.g. Tony Blair was once photographed on holiday in a pair of **bilious** *swimming shorts*

---

bilk (verb)
= **to take money (from someone) using deceitful methods** *bilk is a variant of 'balk', a mid 17th-century English word meaning 'to spoil one's opponent's score in the card game of cribbage'*

e.g. The young Errol Flynn was sacked from his job as a clerk when he **bilked** money from petty cash to bet on a horse

bipartisan (adj.)
= **involving the agreement of two political parties usually at loggerheads** *from the Latin bi-: two, and partire: to part*

e.g. The creation of animal-human hybrid embryos for scientific research received **bipartisan** support from the then opposing leaders David Cameron and Gordon Brown

blandishment (noun)
= **a pleasing utterance to persuade someone to do something** from the Latin *blandus*: soft, smooth, from *blandiri*: to flatter

e.g. Fidel Castro persuaded Graham Greene to campaign on his behalf against the US government by directing **blandishments** towards the writer

blitzkrieg (noun)
= **a short but devastatingly effective military campaign** *for etymology, see box below*

e.g. Mike Tyson would often go several rounds without troubling an opponent before unleashing a **blitzkrieg** of punches that would finish them off in seconds

---

blitzkrieg means in German 'a lightning war'.

After a poor performance in World War I, Germany's military leaders refined their tactics, resulting in the ***blitzkrieg*** *concept that was used to such effect in World War II. The blitzkrieg consisted of a co-ordinated onslaught by planes, tanks and infantry, which simultaneously converged on one weak point of enemy lines with the aim of 'breaking through'. The goal was to instil terror in the enemy; for this reason the planes were fitted with propellers known to make extra noise.*

There is no record of the term ***blitzkrieg*** *in German military handbooks; in fact the term was coined by a journalist from* **The Times** *in 1939 to describe Germany's invasion of Poland. Today we continue to use the phrase to refer to any short but effective attack by one person on another.*

---

boulevardier (noun)
= **a socialite who is well-off and fashionable** from the French *boulevardier*: a person who frequents *boulevards* (which are wide city streets lined with trees, commonly found in more gentrified areas)

e.g. With a long list of celebrity friends, hotel heiress Paris Hilton is a noted **boulevardier**

bowdlerise (verb)
= **to cut out material considered unsuitable (from a work), especially with the result that the work becomes less powerful** *for etymology, see box below*

e.g. The censors **bowdlerised** the film *The Texas Chainsaw Massacre* before clearing it for release

---

bowdlerise derives from the name of Dr Thomas Bowdler (1754–1825), who in 1818 published a severely edited version of Shakespeare.

As he lived in a prudish age, Bowdler knew that there would be a market for a sanitised version of Shakespeare's work – a version suitable for women and children. Bowdler called his work The Family Shakespeare *and it was a big success.*

Today, we continue to refer to any work of art that has been pared down by a censor as being **bowdlerised**.

---

braggadocio (noun)
= **boasting and swaggering** *for etymology, see box opposite*

e.g. In his last film, *The Misfits*, Clark Gable insisted on doing his own stunts, including being dragged by a horse; this **braggadocio** led to a fatal heart attack

braggadocio derives from the name of Braggadocchio, a character in a poem called **The Faerie Queene** *that was published in 1590 by Edmund Spenser to celebrate Queen Elizabeth I.*

*The character Braggadocchio was famous for his boasting and vain nature and we still use the word **braggadocio** today to refer to any behaviour of this type.*

bulwark (noun)

= **something or someone that acts as a barricade** from the Middle High German *Bollwerk*, from *Bohle*: plank, and *Werk*: work; *a bulwark literally means 'a defensive wall'*

e.g. Cherie Blair found her husband's soothing comments a **bulwark** against harsh articles by journalists

bumptious (adj.)

= **offensively self-assertive** from the 19th century, derived from 'bump'; a humorous coinage on the pattern of 'fractious'

e.g. Chat show hosts cannot afford to be too **bumptious**, as they must allow their guests to dominate the conversation

burlesque (noun)

= **humour resulting from a comically exaggerated portrayal; OR a variety show involving undressing to music** from the Italian *burlesco*, from *burla*: mockery

e.g. Some comedians make a living out of the **burlesque** by imitating the voices of politicians

Byronic (adj.)

= *(of a man)* **dark and enigmatic in an attractive way** *for etymology, see box below*

e.g. In the film *Four Weddings and a Funeral*, Hugh Grant plays a **Byronic** lothario

---

Byronic derives from the name of Lord Byron (1788–1824), an English poet famously described by Lady Caroline Lamb as 'mad, bad and dangerous to know' because of his womanising and risk-loving nature.

It is appropriate then that Byron is today best known for his poem Don Juan, *which describes the exploits of a serial philanderer; when we use the word* **Byronic** *today, we evoke Lord Byron's dangerous air that so enthralled women.*

Byzantine (adj.)

= *(of an administration)* **highly complex and sometimes devious** *for etymology, see box below*

e.g. Most people find the UK government's tax system to be **Byzantine**

The **Byzantine** *Empire was the name for the Roman Empire between the 4th and 15th centuries AD.*

The Byzantine Empire was vast and sprawling and hence required a complex system of government, with thousands of different types of bureaucrats, all wearing different hats and outfits to denote their rank; it is no surprise that, in such a competitive environment, the most successful politicians were marked by their deviousness. Today, when we refer to an administration as **Byzantine**, *we evoke this sense of unfathomable complexity as well as the deviousness of its creators.*

cabal (noun)
= **a secret political group** from the French *cabal*: society

e.g. On the many occasions that his leadership was under threat, Gordon Brown moved quickly to disband the **cabal** responsible

cadence (noun)
= **a drop in the intensity of the voice at the end of a sentence** from the Latin *cadere*: to fall; the collection of notes comprising the close of a musical phrase

e.g. You can listen to Dame Judi Dench for hours because her voice is full of soothing **cadences**

cadre (noun)
= **a small group of people trained for a specific role** from the Latin *quadrus*: a square

e.g. The SAS is an elite **cadre** of army troops

callisthenics (noun)
= **gymnastic exercises which have as their aims fitness and grace** from the Greek *kallos*: beauty, and *sthenos*: strength

e.g. The biggest-selling fitness video of all time, *Jane Fonda's Workout*, shows the actress performing her **callisthenics** regime

callow (adj.)
= *(of a young person)* **naive** from the Latin *calvus*: bald

e.g. The 11-year-old Audrey Hepburn carried messages for the Dutch Resistance hidden in her shoes: she looked so **callow** that the Nazis never suspected her

cant (noun)
= **language specific to one group of people and looked down on by others; OR a hypocritical sermon** from the Latin *cantare*: to sing

e.g. At the Oscars, the woman who wins 'Best Actress' usually embarks on the effusive **cant** that is customary at such events

carapace (noun)
= **a protective shell** from the French *carapace*: a tortoise shell; *a carapace is literally 'the hard upper shell of a turtle'*

e.g. People who are bullied have to develop a **carapace** in order to survive

careen (verb)
= **to move fast but in an uncontrolled way in one direction** from the Latin *carina*: a keel (which is a kind of ship)

e.g. James Dean died when a car **careened** into his own on State Route 46 in California

carious (adj.)
= *(of teeth and bone)* **rotted away** from the Latin *caries*: decay

e.g. When talking, Oscar Wilde used to put one hand over his mouth to disguise his **carious** teeth from his interlocutor

carnivalesque (adj.)
= **involving a fun and uproarious mix** *for etymology, see box below*

e.g. After England won the 2003 Rugby World Cup, a **carnivalesque** atmosphere reigned in London

---

*The word **carnivalesque** is the adjective from the noun 'carnival', which is a period of celebration that takes place in Roman Catholic countries in the weeks before Lent (i.e. in January and February).*

*For Catholics, Lent is a time of austerity when luxuries such as meat are renounced – hence the etymology of the word **carnival** that derives from the Latin carne vale, meaning 'farewell to meat', as the carnival is the last chance to celebrate and indulge oneself before Lent's rigours.*

*Processions and masked dancers characterise a carnival and when we use the word **carnivalesque**, we refer to this spirit of celebration.*

Cassandra (noun)
= **someone who correctly predicts disaster but whom no one listens to** *for etymology, see box below*

e.g. no one would listen to the few economists who in 2007 warned the world was about to enter a recession; but these **Cassandras** sadly proved only too accurate in their predictions

---

Cassandra was in Greek mythology the daughter of the Trojan king Priam. Apollo took a shine to the beautiful Cassandra and gave her the power of prophecy. When it became clear that Cassandra did not return Apollo's love,

Apollo became angry and turned his gift to her into a curse by causing her prophecies, though still true, to be ignored by everyone.

*Today, we continue to describe as a **Cassandra** anyone who correctly predicts a catastrophe – such as the recent credit crunch – but is not listened to.*

caustic (adj.)
= **sarcastic in a particularly angry way** from the Greek *kaustos*: combustible; *caustic literally means 'able to corrode organic matter by chemical action'*

e.g. Judy Garland, star of *The Wizard of Oz*, gave her own mother the **caustic** title 'the real-life Wicked Witch of the West'

cavalcade (noun)
= **a formal line of people or objects moving together** *for etymology, see box below*

e.g. At Elvis Presley's funeral, the **cavalcade** included 16 white Cadillacs and one white hound dog

---

*A **cavalcade** literally refers to a procession of people on horseback who gather to commemorate an historical event; the riders often travel huge distances in the process. The etymology of the word **cavalcade** reflects this equine connection, deriving as it does from the Italian 'cavalcare', meaning 'to ride'.*

*For example, hundreds of riders gather in Chihuahua in Mexico every year and embark on a journey across the country, which lasts several weeks and culminates in their entering the US; this **cavalcade** is to re-enact a Mexican general's brief invasion of the US in 1916.*

---

caveat emptor (phrase)
= **the principle that it is the buyer alone who is responsible for ensuring that something purchased is of good quality** from the Latin *caveat emptor*: let the buyer beware

e.g. When a customer drives off with an old car that has been made to look like a new one, the car salesman thinks to himself: '**caveat emptor**'

cerulean (adj.)
= *(of a colour)* **blue like a cloudless sky** from the Latin *caeruleus*: sky blue

e.g. It is enjoyable to go for a stroll when the sun is bright and the sky **cerulean**

ceteris paribus (adv.)
= **assuming other conditions remain unchanged** from the Latin *ceteris paribus*: with other things being the same

e.g. Rising unemployment will, **ceteris paribus**, lead to a weaker economy

chicanery (noun)
= **deception** from the French *chicaner*: to quibble

e.g. Investors did not become aware of Bernard Madoff's **chicanery** until it was too late

chimera (noun)
= **a thing that is forever desired but not achievable** *for etymology, see box opposite*

e.g. Due to our responsibilities to others, we must all accept that absolute personal liberty is a **chimera**

chimera derives from the Greek word khimaira, *which was in Greek mythology a monster that had a lion's head, a goat's body, and a serpent's tail.*

Such an animal does not of course exist in reality – and today chimera *retains this sense of something that is an impossible dream that will never become a reality.*

chrysalis (noun)
= **a stage involving preparation** from the Greek *khrusos*: gold (because of the golden colour of the pupae of some species); *a chrysalis literally means 'the discarded hard outer case of a quiescent insect pupa of a butterfly'*

e.g. The young Al Pacino spent a year with two aunts whose deafness forced him to gesticulate; this proved a good **chrysalis** for his extravagant acting style

cinéaste (noun)
= **a lover of films** from the French *ciné* (from *cinéma*), on the pattern of *enthousiaste*: enthusiast

e.g. Before writing scripts, Quentin Tarantino worked in a DVD rental store, which was the perfect job for a **cinéaste** like him

cipher (noun)
= **a person who is insignificant** from the Old French *cifre*, based on the Arabic *sifr*: zero

e.g. As a constitutional monarch, the Queen does not interfere with the running of government but she does work hard for the country and is no mere **cipher**

circumlocutory (adj.)

= **using many words when there is no need** from the Latin *circumlocutio*, from *circum-*: around, and *locutio*: speech

e.g. A standard conversation with Fidel Castro is reported to last hours because the Cuban leader is so **circumlocutory**

cirrus cloud (phrase)

= **a cloud with threads around it** from the Latin *cirrus*: a curl

e.g. Einstein had white hair that surrounded his head like a **cirrus cloud**

clarion call (phrase)

= **a call for action** from the Latin *clarus*: clear; *a clarion call literally refers to a blast from a 'clarion', which is a shrill war trumpet*

e.g. Barack Obama's election campaign speeches included a **clarion call** for change

cleave (verb)

= **to become extremely emotionally involved with (someone)** from the Old English *clifian*: to stick

e.g. To fall in love at first sight is to **cleave** instantly to another person

---

*Note that **cleave** has a secondary meaning (which is the direct opposite of the one above):*

– to split something asunder, using force

from the Old English 'cleofan': to split

*e.g. In winter people use axes to **cleave** wood for the fire*

---

climacteric (noun)
= **a period when events of huge significance occur** from the Greek *klimakter*: a critical period

e.g. The time surrounding the invasion of Iraq was the **climacteric** of Tony Blair's Prime Ministership

coda (noun)
= **an ending** from the Latin *cauda*: tail

e.g. Elvis Presley received more than 19,000 uppers and downers from his doctor during the two years before he died: this was a sad **coda** to the star's life

compère (noun)
= **the main presenter of a show, responsible for introducing others** from the French *compère*: a godfather

e.g. When his mother's voice gave out, the five-year-old Charlie Chaplin finished her song after being ushered on by the **compère**

concatenation (noun)
= **a series of things that are linked as if in a chain** from the Latin *con-*: together, and *catena*: chain; *a concatenation literally means 'the action of linking things together in a chain'*

e.g. Andy Warhol sometimes produced paintings by having his dog urinate on the canvas; the critics lauded the resulting **concatenations** of yellow

concomitant (noun)

= **a phenomenon that goes hand in hand with something else** from the Latin *concomitari*, from *con-*: together with, and *comitari*: to accompany (from the Latin *comes*: companion)

e.g. Diseases such as psoriasis are often **concomitants** to stress

conflation (noun)

= **the act of melding two or more ideas into one** from the Latin *conflare*: to fuse, from *con-*: together, and *flare*: to blow

e.g. When Ben Affleck and Jennifer Lopez were an item, journalists used to refer to the couple by the **conflation** of 'Bennifer'

congeries (noun)

= **a messy collection** from the Latin *congeries*: a heap, from *congerere*: to heap up

e.g. The competitors on the TV show *Big Brother* are from a **congeries** of backgrounds

congruous (adj.)

= **harmonious** from the Latin *congruere*: to agree

e.g. It seems **congruous** that William Shakespeare died on the 23rd of April – for that is also the day he was born

conquistador (noun)

= **a person who sets out in search of adventure** *for etymology, see box opposite*

e.g. Society's double standards mean that promiscuous men are lauded as **conquistadors** whilst promiscuous women are viewed as sluts

conquistador means 'conqueror' in both Spanish and Portuguese.

Following Christopher Columbus's discovery of the New World in 1492, Spanish conquistadors took control of most of America, placing it under Spanish rule.

*Today, the term **conquistador** is used to denote a conqueror of any kind.*

consigliere (noun)
= **someone who advises** from the Italian *consigliere*: adviser

e.g. Before Henry VIII turned on him and chopped off his head, Sir Thomas More was **consigliere** to the king

continuum (noun)
= **a continuous sequence in which adjacent elements are very similar to each other, but the extremes are polar opposites** from the Latin *continuus*: uninterrupted

e.g. Alfred Kinsey believed that human sexuality forms a **continuum**, with complete heterosexuality at one end and complete homosexuality at the other

contrail (noun)
= **the streak of white that a plane leaves behind it**
contrail is an abbreviation of the 1940s expression 'condensation trail'

e.g. The jet passed overhead, leaving a **contrail** in the sky

contumely (noun)

= **insulting treatment** from the Latin *contumelia*: an insult, from *con-* (an intensifying prefix), and *tumere*: to swell up

e.g. A judge will not stand for **contumely** from a witness in court

cornucopia (noun)

= **an overflowing supply of pleasant things** from the Latin *cornu copiae*: horn of plenty; a *cornucopia* literally means 'a symbol of plenty consisting of a goat's horn overflowing with flowers and fruit'; for etymology, see box below

e.g. Guests at weddings can expect to be served a **cornucopia** of food

---

cornucopia means in Latin 'a horn of plenty' (cornu copiae); *from the 5th century BC, this was a symbol of food and abundance.*

The following Greek myth explains why it is that a goat's horn has become associated with a surfeit of good things.

When the god Zeus was young, he used to play with a goat, whose horn he broke off one day by accident; to make amends, the god returned the horn to the goat, but in an improved form, for it was imbued with magical powers that meant whoever possessed it got whatever they wished for.

Hence the horn came to be depicted by the Greeks as bursting with fruits and flowers and other treats that people desired; today we continue to use the word **cornucopia** *to refer to any bountiful display of food and goodies.*

---

corollary (noun)

= **something that naturally follows** from the Latin *corollarium*: money paid for a garland

e.g. People who have cataracts in their eyes literally see red: in fact the reddish tone of Monet's paintings is a **corollary** of his suffering from the condition

coruscating (adj.)

= *(of light or of humour)* **sparkling** from the Latin *coruscare*: to glitter

e.g. American wit H. L. Mencken once said, 'On one issue at least, men and women agree: they both distrust women'. What **coruscating** humour!

costive (adj.)

= *(of someone's character)* **niggardly**; *(of speech or movement)* **slow** from the Old French *costivé*: constipated (itself derived from the Latin *constipatus*: pressed together); *costive literally means 'constipated'*

e.g. Henry VIII became obese in his old age and later portraits of the monarch show him looking positively **costive**

coterie (noun)

= **a small group of people with a common goal** from the French *cotier*: an organisation of peasants holding land owned by a feudal lord

e.g. Elvis Presley was accompanied everywhere by the 'Memphis Mafia': his **coterie** of bodyguards and helpers

coup de grâce (noun)
= **a fatal blow that finishes off a wounded animal** from the French *coup de grâce*: a stroke of grace

e.g. For a discontented wife, the discovery that her husband has been unfaithful is usually the **coup de grâce** for the marriage

covey (noun)
= **a small crowd of people** from the Old French *covée*: a brood; *a 'covey' literally means 'a small flock of birds'*

e.g. As Tom Cruise arrived at the premiere of *Mission Impossible*, a **covey** of photographers snapped away

cowlick (noun)
= **a clump of hair at the back of the head that refuses to be straightened but sticks up straight as if licked by a cow**

e.g. The hairdo of cartoon character Tintin consists of one giant **cowlick**

crapulent (adj.)
= **nauseous due to overindulgence** from the Latin *crapula*: inebriation

e.g. The wide girth of the older Marlon Brando spoke of a man who had enjoyed many a **crapulent** evening

craven (adj.)
= **so timid as to be cowardly** from the Old French *cravante*, past participle of *cravanter*: to crush

e.g. Charlie Chaplin failed to serve in World War I – not because he was **craven**, but because the army rejected him for being too small

cri de cœur (phrase)
= **a cry from the heart** from the French *cri de cœur*: cry from the heart

e.g. Princess Diana's TV interview with Martin Bashir – when she discussed the constrictions of royal life – was interpreted as a **cri de cœur** by the public

cumulus (noun)
= **a large cloud composed of wispy clumps mixed together** from the Latin *cumulus*: heap

e.g. On entering the **cumulus**, the pilot of the helicopter couldn't see a thing

cupola (noun)
= **a small dome that sits on top of a roof of a larger dome** from the Latin *cupula*: small cask

e.g. Adorning the curved roof of the main dome of St Paul's Cathedral is a celebrated **cupola**

cursive (adj./noun)
= *(of script)* **written in joined up handwriting** (adj.) /
handwriting that is joined up (noun) from the Latin
currere: to run

e.g. As a boy Hitchcock was obsessed with locomotives:
the floor of his room was strewn with train timetables
copied out in primitive **cursive**

de facto (phrase)

= **in fact** (*regardless of whether this is the proper state of affairs*) from the Latin *de facto*: of fact

e.g. Colonel Gadaffi has been the **de facto** leader of Libya since a coup in 1969

defray (verb)

= **to give money to cover (an expense)** from the French *defrayer*, from *de-* (expressing removal), and *frai*: cost

e.g. If you are unemployed, the government will pay you a jobseeker's allowance to **defray** your outgoings

deleterious (adj.)

= **destructive** from the Greek *deleterios*: noxious

e.g. Serial killer Fred West had violent rages, resulting from a motorbike accident that was **deleterious** to his brain

Delphic (adj.)
= *(of a pronouncement)* **purposefully unclear** *for etymology, see box opposite*

e.g. After being charged for kicking out at opposition fans, footballer Eric Cantona called a press conference to deliver the following **Delphic** pronouncement: *'when the seagulls follow the trawler, it is because they think sardines will be thrown into the sea'*

Delphic has its derivation in the ancient Greek oracle at Delphi, whose priestess was said to have the power of prediction; however, her pronouncements were so ambiguous that it was very hard to work out what she meant.

For example, the oracle once warned a warrior called Lysander to watch out for: 'a serpent...craftily creeping up behind you...'

Lysander was presumably ever alert for snakes after that but in the end was killed by a man who was standing behind him at the time and who had a snake on his shield – so the oracle's warning, although truthful in a way, wasn't really helpful.

Today we use the term *Delphic* to evoke any pronouncement that is similarly hard to understand.

demimonde (noun)
= **a group of people on the periphery of society** for *etymology, see box below*

e.g. Unlicensed cab drivers form part of the **demimonde** of illegal workers in the UK

demimonde is a French expression meaning 'half-world'; in 19th-century France the term referred to those women who were shunned by society because they lived off their wealthy lovers to whom they were not married.

Today, society is more tolerant of such situations and so the term *demimonde* no longer refers to women in this position, but continues to be used of people who are on the fringes of society, such as workers who are in the UK illegally.

demotic (adj.)
= **relating to everyday language** from the Greek
demotikos: popular

e.g. Dan Brown writes forcefully in **demotic** English and
this in part explains the huge success of his book *The Da
Vinci Code*

dénouement (noun)
= **the climax of several actions, when the outcome
becomes clear** from the French *dénouer*: to unknot

e.g. Superman always triumphs over Lex Luthor in the
dénouement of the comic strips

depredation (noun)
= **an act of looting** from the Latin *depraedari*: to plunder

e.g. After some would-be blackmailers attempted a
depredation of Charlie Chaplin's corpse, his family
reburied his body under six feet of concrete

deracinate (verb)
= **to take something by the roots and tear it out; to
alienate someone from their natural environment** from
the French *deraciner*, from *de-* (expressing removal), and
racine: root

e.g. Model Claudia Schiffer, who was born in Germany
but now lives in England, is always photographed smiling:
she never looks **deracinated**

desultory (adj.)
= **jumping from one thing to another** from the Latin
desultor: vaulter, from the verb *desilire*: to jump down

e.g. The inebriated diner can have difficulty following a **desultory** dinner party conversation

deus ex machina (noun)
= **an event that comes out of the blue and changes the outcome of a story** *for etymology, see box below*

e.g. In the Mel Gibson film *Apocalypto*, the hero is saved from human sacrifice by the **deus ex machina** of a solar eclipse

---

deus ex machina derives from the Greek term theos ek mekhane *(meaning 'god from the machinery') and referred to those actors who, because they represented gods, were suspended above the stage in Greek theatres.*

Eventually these actors would be lowered down and intervene in the events on the stage, thus bringing about the play's ending.

Today, we continue to use the term deus ex machina to refer to any device that appears from nowhere to end a film, play or novel.

---

dialectic (noun)
= **the contradiction between two opposing forces viewed as the determining factor in their continuing interaction**
from the Greek *dialektike*: debate

e.g. The tension between the human tendency to sin and the desire for salvation is the **dialectic** that fascinated novelist Graham Greene

diaspora (noun)
= **the scattering of any people outside their homeland; OR the people who have been thus scattered** from the Greek *dia-*: across, and *speirein*: to scatter (hence *diaspeirein*: to disperse)

e.g. The 21-year-old Arnold Schwarzenegger came to the US in the 1960s: he was part of a **diaspora** from Europe at that time

dichotomy (noun)
= **a contrast between two things that are polar opposites** from the Greek *dikhotomia*, from *dikho-*: in two, and *tomia*: cutting (from *temnein*: to cut)

e.g. Bestselling authors like John Grisham are used to the **dichotomy** of being very popular with the public but sometimes unpopular with the critics

Dickensian (adj.)
= **bringing to mind the novels of Charles Dickens (especially in evoking the themes of poverty and exploitation)** *for etymology, see box below*

e.g. In one **Dickensian** scene from Roald Dahl's book *Matilda*, a cruel headmistress beats the girl Matilda

---

Dickensian refers to the novels of Charles Dickens, which were works of social commentary, as the author was committed to exposing poverty in Victorian society.

The publicity unleashed by Dickens's novel Oliver Twist *(1838), for example, led to the eventual dismantlement of a slum called Jacob's Island that was the basis for the story.*

*Today we continue to use the term **Dickensian** to refer to any work that draws attention to poverty and social inequality.*

dictum (noun)
= a short statement that expresses a universal truth; OR a pronouncement from an official source from the Latin *dictum*: something said, neuter past participle of *dicere*: to say

e.g. Actor Warren Beatty is discreet about his romances, citing the **dictum**: 'Obviously my sex life is not mine alone to talk about'

didactic (adj.)
= in the style of a patronising teacher from the Greek *didaktikos*, from *didaskein*: to teach

e.g. Readers prefer novels that have a subtle message rather than a **didactic** ending

diktat (noun)
= an order imposed by a ruler despite objections from his people from the Latin *dictatum*: something dictated

e.g. Tyrants issue **diktats** on a whim

dilatory (adj.)
= slow to take action (often purposefully so) from the Latin *dilatorius*: delaying

e.g. Alfred Hitchcock was awarded a knighthood but died before the Queen could present it to him because he was so **dilatory** in arranging to receive it

Dionysian (adj.)
= **relating to the realms of sexual and emotional gratification** *for etymology, see box below*

e.g. Hugh Hefner, owner of *Playboy* magazine, is known for his parties that the media depict as **Dionysian**

---

*Dionysian derives from the name of Dionysus, who in Greek mythology was the god of wine and ecstasy: hence the word **Dionysian** today refers to displays of intoxication and sensual indulgence.*

Note that Dionysus had a brother, Apollo, who was the exact opposite; when we describe someone as 'Apollonian', we mean that they embody Apollo's calm and disciplined nature.

*(Bacchus was the name given to Dionysus by the Romans, see **bacchanalian**.)*

---

dirge (noun)
= **a lament for the dead** from the Latin *dirige!* (imperative): direct!

e.g. At Michael Jackson's funeral, the mourners were moved to tears by the **dirge** sung by Stevie Wonder

disburse (verb)
= *(of money)* **to pay out** from the Old French *desbourser*, from *des-* (expressing removal), and *bourse*: purse

e.g. The government collects taxes then **disburses** this money, directing it to public services such as the NHS

disport oneself (verb)
= **to enjoy oneself without inhibitions** from the Old French *desporter*, from *des-*: away, and *porter*: to carry

e.g. In advertisements for holidays, models are often pictured **disporting themselves** on sunlit beaches

disquisition (noun)
= **a long speech on a topic** from the Latin *disquisitio*: investigation, based on *quaerere*: to seek

e.g. Martin Luther King was renowned for his public **disquisitions** on civil rights

dissemble (verb)
= **to hide one's true motives** from the Latin *dissimulare*: to disguise

e.g. When someone asks 'How are you?', people who have the flu often **dissemble** and say 'Fine, thanks' rather than discuss their ailment

dissimulate (verb)
= **to hide one's true thoughts** from the Latin *dissimulare*: to conceal

e.g. Faced with a large hotel bill, Errol Flynn feigned appendicitis: he had no compunction about **dissimulating**

dissipate (verb)
= **to disappear (via dispersal); OR to cause to disappear**
from the Latin *dissipare*: to scatter

e.g. Once he'd stopped boxing, Mike Tyson found an
alternative way to **dissipate** his energy: by working out in
the gym

distend (verb)
= **to swell due to a force from inside** from the Latin *distendere*: to stretch out, from *dis-*: apart, and *tendere*: to stretch

e.g. When pregnant with twins, actress Angelina Jolie had a noticeably **distended** belly

diuretic (noun)
= **a drug that causes one to pass water more frequently** from the Greek *dia*: through, and *ouron*: urine (hence *diourein*: to urinate)

e.g. Alcohol and coffee are the most commonly used **diuretics**

doctrinaire (adj.)
= **stubbornly insisting on applying a doctrine** from the Latin *doctrina*: teaching, from *docere*: to teach

e.g. Detractors of the Catholic Church say it is **doctrinaire** in sexual matters

Doric (adj.)
= **relating to a classical order of architecture, characterised by a thick grooved column, topped by a rounded moulding and then a square** from the Greek *Dorios*: of Doris; *which refers to the people of Doris who entered central Greece from the north in c.1100 BC, and later colonised southern Italy*

e.g. In the grounds of English country estates, you often find streams with **Doric** temples nearby

doublethink

doublethink (noun)
= **the ability to simultaneously believe in two ideas that contradict each other, while wilfully ignoring this contradiction** *for etymology, see box below*

e.g. Critics say the Chinese government's statement – that 'China's Internet is open and managed in accordance with the law' – is an example of **doublethink**

---

doublethink is a concept invented by George Orwell in his novel Nineteen Eighty-Four. *(See* **Orwellian** *for more information about this author.)*

Nineteen Eighty-Four *describes a totalitarian government which exercises control over its subjects via propaganda. Yet the risk remains for the ruling regime that the disgust felt by its own officials at this use of propaganda might lead to the collapse of the system. This is the reason the ruling regime uses reality control to ensure everyone – even its own officials – remains wilfully ignorant of contradictions within the regime's use of propaganda.*

One of the reality control devices that officials are encouraged to use is **doublethink**, *which, Orwell tells us, is the ability to hold 'two contradictory beliefs in one's mind simultaneously' while believing both of them to be correct. An example in the book is when civil servants rewrite government history and are then able to believe wholeheartedly in this new version of history that they themselves have just created.*

Today, we use the word **doublethink** *to refer to any instance of someone wilfully ignoring contradictions in a belief system.*

---

dovish (adj.)
= *(of a person)* **advocating peace** *for etymology, see box below*

e.g. Ghandi did so much to promote peace that he is still considered the most **dovish** politician of all time

---

dovish is an adjective deriving from 'dove', which is traditionally seen as a bird of peace due to its white feathers and cooing voice; hence, for example, the Christian faith's depiction of the Holy Spirit as a dove.

*Today, when we call someone **dovish**, we mean that person advocates peaceful policies in foreign affairs.*

*(For the word to describe someone who is the opposite of dovish, see **hawkish** see p.90.)*

---

ductile (adj.)
= **able to be guided** from the Latin *ductilis*, from *duct-*: led (from the verb *ducere*: to lead)

e.g. Bing Crosby used to pin back his cauliflower ears with gum: his ears were sufficiently **ductile** to allow this

dyad (noun)
= **two individuals that are viewed as a pair** from the Greek *duas*: two

e.g. Psychologists spend much time discussing the parent-child **dyad**

---

dyspeptic (adj.)
= **having indigestion; OR having the irritability that results from indigestion** from the Greek *duspeptos*: difficult to digest

e.g. After a ten-course meal, most people look **dyspeptic**

dystopia (noun)
= **an imagined place that is nightmarish** from the Greek *dys-*: bad, and *topos*: place

e.g. In his documentary film *An Inconvenient Truth*, Al Gore warns us that we face **dystopia** unless we arrest global warming

edict (noun)
= **an order from someone in office** from the Latin *edicere*, from *e-*: out, and *dicere*: to say, tell

e.g. 'Drink to me, drink to my health – you know I can't drink any more' was the last **edict** uttered by Pablo Picasso to his friends before he died

effluent (noun)
= **waste in liquid form that is emitted into a river** from the Latin *effluere*: to flow out

e.g. Effluent from factories contaminates rivers

effulgent (adj.)
= *(of a light)* **shining strongly; OR** *(of a person's expression)* **emanating happiness** from the Latin *effulgere*: to shine brightly, from *ex-*: out, and *fulgere*: to shine

e.g. Mother Theresa's kindness found expression in her **effulgent** face

egalitarian (adj.)
= **relating to the premise that all people are equal** from the French *égal*: equal

e.g. Social activists press for an **egalitarian** society

egregious (adj.)
= **so bad as to stand out** from the Latin e-: out, and *grex*:
flock; *egregious* literally means 'standing out from the flock
because the thing being described is so bad'

e.g. In September 1955, James Dean died from **egregious**
injuries sustained in a car crash: his head was almost
severed from his body

eldorado (noun)
= **an imaginary place full of gold sought in South America by 16th-century explorers; OR a lifelong goal** *for etymology, see box below*

e.g. In the 19th century, many Europeans left to settle in the US, which they viewed as **eldorado**

---

eldorado – which means 'the golden one' (El Dorado) *in Spanish – refers to a mythical city of gold that the 16th-century Spanish* **conquistadors** *(see p. 36) were told existed in the newly discovered America.*

Spurred on by assurances from captive Indians that El Dorado overflowed with gold and precious gemstones, groups of Spaniards went out to find this place – but in vain, with many of them dying from diseases and attacks by the natives.

Today, we use the word **eldorado** *to signify a place where wealth can be acquired quickly (doubtless the founders of the world's biggest websites would describe the Internet as an eldorado).* **Eldorado** *can also be used to refer to a lifelong ambition (such as attaining happiness) and, in this way, it is similar to the word* **Shangri-La** *(see p. 184).*

---

elegiac (adj.)
= *(of a work of art)* **like a lament** from the Greek *elegos*: a lament

e.g. The film *Schindler's List*, which covers the atrocities committed by the Nazis, has an **elegiac** tone

elliptical (adj.)
= *(of speech)* **lacking key words (but the sense can be worked out from the context)** from the Greek *elleiptikos*: defective, from *elleipein*: to leave out

e.g. In the film *ET*, it is easy to understand phrases such as 'ET go home' even though they are **elliptical**

elucidate (verb)
= **to explain (something) clearly** from the Latin *elucidare*: to make clear, from *e-*: out, and *lucidus*: light

e.g. In his book *A Brief History of Time* (1988), Stephen Hawking uses simple language to **elucidate** the subject of black holes

emaciated (adj.)
= **to be unusually lean** from the Latin *emaciare*, from *e-* (expressing a change of state), and *macies*: leanness

e.g. Due to a meagre diet most homeless people look **emaciated**

embonpoint (noun)
= **plumpness of person** from the French *en bon point*: in good condition; embonpoint is a euphemism for fatness

e.g. Towards the end of his life Marlon Brando grew depressed and his **embonpoint** increased dramatically

emetic (noun)
= **a substance that brings about vomiting** from the Greek *emein*: to vomit

e.g. The emperor Nero tried to keep his weight down by using **emetics**

éminence grise (noun)

= **a person who wields considerable power even though they have no official role** *for etymology, see box below*

e.g. When Tony Blair was in power, the media depicted his unelected adviser Alistair Campbell as the **éminence grise** of the Labour Party.

> **éminence grise** *is a French expression literally meaning 'grey eminence'.*
>
> *The reason we use this term to describe a person who exerts a powerful but behind-the-scenes influence is because the first example of the controlling types to which this word refers was the grey-cloaked Père Joseph (1577–1638), who was the private secretary who controlled Cardinal Richelieu (who himself controlled King Louis XIII, the nominal ruler of France).*

endemic (adj.)

= **characteristic of people belonging to one particular area** from the Greek *endemos*: native, based on *demos*: people

e.g. Roger Federer epitomises the cool precision **endemic** to the Swiss

enervate (verb)

= **to weaken (someone)** from the Latin *enervare*: to weaken (by extraction of the sinews)

e.g. People involved in even minor car crashes feel **enervated** for weeks afterwards

enmity (noun)
= **hostility towards someone or something** from the Latin *inimicus*: enemy

e.g. When somebody accused him of being a vandal because he was signing copies of his own novels in a bookshop, Stephen King felt no **enmity**; he knew it was a simple misunderstanding

ennui (noun)
= **the kind of dissatisfaction that arises when nothing exciting has happened for a while** from the French *ennui*: boredom

e.g. Teenagers are moody because the chemical changes in their bodies ensure they feel **ennui** more than the rest of us

ephemeron (noun)
= **something that is short-lived** from the Greek *ephemeros*: lasting only a day

e.g. Charlie Chaplin is still well-known today: his fame was no **ephemeron**

epithet (noun)
= **a phrase that describes someone** from the Greek *epitheton*, neuter of *epithetos*: attributed

e.g. In his bodybuilding days, Arnold Schwarzenegger's powerful physique meant that he was known by the **epithet** of 'The Austrian Oak'

eponymous (adj.)
= *(of a person)* **giving their name to something** from the Greek *epi-*: upon, and *onyma*, variant of *onoma*: name

e.g. In the TV series *Columbo*, Peter Falk played the **eponymous** hero detective

ersatz (adj.)
= **used as a poor substitute (for something else)** from
the German, *ersatz*: replacement

e.g. After his marriage to Marilyn Monroe ended,
baseball star Joe DiMaggio pursued lookalikes of his wife;
but he found no joy with these **ersatz** Marilyns

ethereal (adj.)
= **so delicate as to seem otherworldly** from the Greek *aither*: the upper air

e.g. With her thin frame and light hair, Michelle Pfeiffer emits an **ethereal** impression

etiolated (adj.)
= **looking sickly** *for etymology, see box below*

e.g. The Brazilian beauty who calls herself *Giselle* has curves, differentiating her from the average **etiolated** supermodel

---

etiolated was first used to refer to a plant that has become sickly and drawn-looking due to a lack of exposure to light.

*The word **etiolated** then evolved to describe humans in a similarly enfeebled state.*

---

euphonic (adj.)
= **sounding good** from the Greek *eu-*: well, and *phone*: sound

e.g. Elton John is rich because he has produced a series of highly **euphonic** melodies over the years and these have sold well

evanescent (adj.)
= **vanishing fast** from the Latin *evanescere*: to disappear

e.g. The four members of the pop group ABBA got married and then divorced; but sadly these two unions proved to be **evanescent**

eviscerate (verb)
= **to take away the core of something** from the Latin *eviscere*: to disembowel, from *e-*: out, and *viscera*: internal organs

e.g. Director Stanley Kubrick was upset when his film *A Clockwork Orange* was **eviscerated** by the censors

excoriate (verb)
= **to criticise strongly** from the Latin *excoriare*: to skin, from *ex-*: out, and *corium*: skin; *excoriate literally means 'to remove part of the surface of the skin'*

e.g. Peter Sutcliffe, the Yorkshire Ripper, is **excoriated** for his horrific murders of women

exculpate (verb)
= **to prove (that someone is) not guilty** from the Latin *ex-*: out, and *culpare*: to blame

e.g. After a high-profile criminal trial, O. J. Simpson was **exculpated** of the murder of his wife and her male companion

execrable (adj.)
= **damnable** from the Latin *exsecrari*: to curse (the inverse of *sacrare*: to dedicate)

e.g. President Mugabe has allowed inflation to escalate; as a consequence many Zimbabweans live in **execrable** poverty

exemplar (noun)
= **an outstanding example** from the Latin *exemplum*: a sample, imitation

e.g. In the UK, the Queen is a leading **exemplar** of selfless duty

exigent (adj.)

= **demanding** from the Latin *exigere*: to demand

e.g. After performing, Pavarotti could barely speak because the physical demands of singing were so **exigent**

expatiate (verb)

= *(of speech)* **to elaborate** from the Latin *exspatiari*: to move beyond one's usual bounds, from *ex-*: out, *spatiari*: to walk

e.g. On the TV show *Richard and Judy*, Judy frequently looked at the camera while Richard **expatiated**

expedient (adj.)

= *(of an action)* **convenient, although possibly morally wrong** from the Latin *expedire*: to extricate, originally by freeing one's feet from being tied up (from *ex-*: out, and *pes, ped-*: foot)

e.g. Critics of David Cameron say he pursues whichever policy is most politically **expedient**

expiate (verb)

= **to make up for (a sin)** from the Latin *expiat-*: appeased by sacrifice, from the verb *expiare*, from *ex-*: out, and *piare*, from *pius*: pious

e.g. Catholics believe that, with prayer and compensatory acts, their sins can be **expiated**

expostulate (verb)

= **to express strong objections** from the Latin *expostulare*: to demand

e.g. When Clark Gable failed his early film auditions because the studios considered his ears too floppy, he would **expostulate** at length

expurgate (verb)
= **to remove matter deemed improper (from a work)**
from the Latin *expurgare*: to thoroughly cleanse, from *ex-*: out, and *purgare*: to cleanse

e.g. Serial womaniser Casanova kept one fingernail especially long so that he could use it to **expurgate** the wax in his ears

extemporise (verb)
= *(of music or a speech)* **to perform spontaneously** from the Latin *ex tempore*: (arising) out of the time

e.g. Louis Armstrong, like every good jazz musician, was capable of **extemporising** at will

extirpate (verb)
= **to rip out by the roots and destroy** from the Latin *exstirpare*, from *ex-*: out, and *stirps*: a stem

e.g. Before his conversion, St Paul was a Roman official devoted to **extirpating** Christianity

F

factious (adj.)
= **relating to a state of conflict within an organisation**
from the Latin *facere*: to do

e.g. After losing the general election the Labour Party
became **factious**; Gordon Brown then quickly resigned

factotum (noun)
= **an employee who performs many tasks** from the Latin
facere: to do, and *totum*: the whole thing

e.g. In his book *A Royal Duty*, Paul Burrell wrote about his
experiences as **factotum** to Princess Diana

fait accompli (phrase)
= **a thing that has been settled before those affected
hear about it** from the French *fait accompli*: accomplished
fact

e.g. When one spouse decides to divorce the other, the
decision is usually presented as a **fait accompli**

fallacy (noun)
= **an incorrect belief** from the Latin *fallacia*: deceit

e.g. There is no evidence that a monster lurks in Loch
Ness – its supposed existence is a **fallacy**

fatuous (adj.)
= **silly** from the Latin *fatuus*: foolish

e.g. Adults may find children's TV programmes **fatuous**

faux-naïf (adj.)
= *(of a work of art or a person)* **naive in an affected way**
from the French *faux*: false, and *naïf*: naive

e.g. In Agatha Christie's novels, detective Miss Marple
lures murderers into a false sense of security with her
faux-naïf manner

febrile (adj.)
= **excited in a nervy way** from the Latin *febris*: fever; *febrile
literally means 'having the symptoms of a fever'*

e.g. In 2008, Lehman Brothers went bust; this made stock
markets **febrile** and share prices fluctuated violently

feckless (adj.)
= **irresponsible and not considering others** from the
northern English dialect *feck* (from *effeck*, variant of
'*effect*')

e.g. A husband who walks out on his pregnant wife is
feckless

fecund (adj.)
= **capable of producing many offspring** from the Latin
fecundus: fruitful

e.g. An hourglass figure is attractive to a man because it
shows that a woman is **fecund**

felicity (noun)
= **a pleasing manner of expression; OR the state of being
happy** from the Latin *felicitas*: happiness

e.g. Barack Obama is famous for speaking with a **felicity**
that no other politician can match

fetid (adj.)
= **smelling very unsavoury** from the Latin *fetere*: to stink

e.g. When investigators opened the door to serial killer Ted Bundy's home, the **fetid** odour of decay assaulted them

fetishise (verb)
= **to develop an irrational devotion to (something)** deriving from the Portuguese word *feitiço*: a charm

e.g. The public **fetishised** the marriage between Princess Diana and Prince Charles because her beauty and his royalty made it a fairytale romance

finagle (verb)
= **to obtain (something) by roguish means** from the Old French *fornier*: to deny

e.g. The media have suggested that Bernard Madoff bought his large houses with money he had **finagled** from others

fissile (adj.)
= **able to be split apart with ease** from the Latin *fiss-*: split (from the verb *findere*: to split, cleave)

e.g. It's hoped that any asteroid approaching the Earth disintegrates before impact: but woe betide humanity if the asteroid is not **fissile**

fissure (noun)

= **a state of discord** from the Latin *fissura*: a cleft, from *findere*: to split, cleave; *a fissure literally means: 'a long narrow opening made by cracking'*

e.g. The writer Dostoevsky gambled away so much money that his wife had to pawn her wedding ring, causing **fissures** in the marriage

flâneur (noun)

= **someone who lounges around** from the French *flâner*: to lounge

e.g. Audrey Hepburn eventually abandoned films in favour of working for UNICEF because she had grown bored of being a **flâneur**

flaxen (adj.)

= *(esp. of hair)* **of the light yellow colour of dressed flax *(which is a type of fibre)*** from the Old English *fleax*: cloth made with linen

e.g. Grace Kelly was renowned for her **flaxen** locks

flotilla (noun)

= **a group moving together** *for etymology, see box below*

e.g. An appearance on Oprah Winfrey's book club ensures an author sells millions more books because of the resulting **flotilla** of interested journalists

---

*A **flotilla** literally means 'a small fleet of ships' in Spanish (**flotilla** being the diminutive of flota, which is the Spanish word for 'a fleet').*

*Within a navy, **flotilla** refers to a group of small warships of the same type, such as submarines or minesweepers.*

*Today, **flotilla** is used most commonly to evoke the image of a small group of people moving around together.*

flummery (noun)
= **hollow compliments** *for etymology, see box below*

e.g. The Queen's speech is popular because people sense the Queen is speaking sincerely: it is far more than **flummery** coming out of her mouth

flummery refers to a pudding consisting of stewed fruit thickened with cornflour. This pudding, gained popularity in the 17th century when it was shaped by a mould and served to applause. However, its taste was bland and unimpressive. So it is that today we continue to use the word 'flummery' to refer to any applause that is meaningless or any praise that is hollow.

folderol (noun)
= **silly fussing** from a nonsense refrain of 'fol-de-rol' in songs from the 19th century

e.g. Barack Obama's daughters looked amused by their father's presidential inauguration ceremony and the attendant **folderol**

folie de grandeur (noun)
= **delusions of grandeur** from the French *folie*: madness, from *de*: of, and *grandeur*: grandeur

e.g. To judge by the number of statues of himself he had built, Saddam Hussein suffered from **folie de grandeur**

foment (verb)
= **to stir up (an unpleasant sentiment)** from the Latin
fomentum: lotion, from *fovere*: to heat

e.g. Billionaire recluse Howard Hughes forbade his staff
from talking to him lest they expel germs in his direction;
this ban **fomented** resentment towards him

fontanelle (noun)
= **a gap between the bones of the skull in an infant,
where the bone has not yet grown over** from the Old
French *fontenelle*, the diminutive of *fontaine*: spring; *this
soft spot of a baby's head was meant to resemble the dent in
the earth where a spring rises*

e.g. You have to make sure when patting a young baby's
head not to press down on the **fontanelle** because it is a
very delicate area

force majeure (phrase)
= **to declare that an event is beyond one's control** from
the French *force majeure*: greater force

e.g. As it was raining incessantly, the organisers of the
cricket match called **force majeure** and cancelled the
game

fountainhead (noun)
= **the source of something** literally referring to a stream's source

e.g. The Beatles remain a **fountainhead** of inspiration for many bands

friable (adj.)
= **easily reduced to powder by the act of crumbling** from the Latin *friare*: to crumble

e.g. You must be careful when arranging dried flowers because they are **friable**

frond (noun)
= **a mass formed by strands of hair** from the Latin *frons, frondis*: a leaf; *a frond literally means 'the leaf of a palm, fern or similar plant'*

e.g. Marilyn Monroe is famous for her blonde hair which tumbled from her head in **fronds**

fulminate against (verb)
= **to express violent protest about something** *for etymology, see box opposite*

e.g. when a wife **fulminates against** her husband, he will often fight back

fulminate derives from the Latin word for lightning (fulmen, fulminis) *and means 'to protest violently'; this is because, in Greek mythology, when the god Zeus became angry, he would hurl a thunderbolt at the person who had irked him.*

The verb **fulminate** *has the following extra meanings:*

– *(of lightning) to flash (in a literal sense – rather than in the metaphorical sense above)*

e.g. When thunder began **to fulminate** *around the house, the children ran into their parents' room*

– *(of a disease) to flare up*

e.g. The doctor operated on the patient at once to cut out the **fulminating** *appendix*

gallimaufry (noun)
= **a messy jumble** from the archaic French *galimafrée*: ragout

e.g. Most high streets are composed of a **gallimaufry** of shops and restaurants

garrulous (adj.)
= **too talkative, especially on matters that are unimportant** from the Latin *garrire*: to chatter

e.g. Einstein's parents at first thought he was retarded because he said nothing until the age of five; but Einstein grew into a **garrulous** adult

gerrymander (verb)
= to redefine an electoral constituency so as to favour one party *for etymology, see box below*

e.g. In the UK, politically neutral organisations define the boundaries of electoral constituencies so as to eliminate the risk of **gerrymandering**

---

*The verb **gerrymander** originated in the early 19th century, arising from the combination of the name of one Governor Elbridge* Gerry *of Massachusetts with the word 'salamander'.*

Seeing that his political party was about to lose an election, Governor Gerry signed a new bill into law that redrew the electoral boundaries to favour his party. This new area happened to include one district that was shaped like a salamander, a creature that looks like a newt.

A journalist noted this resemblance and soon there appeared in The Boston Weekly Messenger *a drawing of a salamander – but with claws and wings added to enhance the impression of evil at work – that was given the title* The Gerry-mander *(to evoke the name of the meddlesome Governor Gerry). Today we continue to use the word **gerrymander** to describe any attempt by a political party to draw up new voting districts to swing the vote its way.*

---

ghoulish (adj.)
= referring to a person obsessed with death and tragedy from the Arabic *gul*: a desert demon believed to rob graves and devour corpses

e.g. The sudden death of someone as well known as Diana Princess of Wales is of interest to everyone, not just to the **ghoulish**

gimcrack (adj.)
= **badly made but attractive in a deceptive way** from the Middle English *gibecrake*: a kind of ornament

e.g. When on holiday people are often tempted to buy **gimcrack** gifts – such as engraved seashells – which they regret purchasing when they get home

gimlet-eyed (adj.)
= **having eyes with a penetrating stare** from the English word, *gimlet*: a tool for boring holes; *gimlet-eyed literally means 'having eyes like a gimlet'*

e.g. One reason for Daniel Craig's being chosen to play James Bond was his **gimlet-eyed** gaze

glacial (adj.)
= **very slow (like the movement of a glacier, which is a mass of slow-moving ice formed from compacted snow on mountains)** from the Latin *glacialis*: icy

e.g. Funeral hearses move at a **glacial** speed compared to normal traffic

---

glacial has the following extra meaning:

– *very cold (which is the other feature of a glacier)*

*e.g. The model Claudia Schiffer is renowned for her **glacial** blue eyes*

---

glib (adj.)
= **talking fluently but without sincerity** from the Dutch, *glibberig*: slippery

e.g. *Jeeves* creator P. G. Wodehouse used to live exclusively in ground floor flats so that he could avoid small talk with **glib** elevator operators

gloaming (noun)
= **the time between daylight and darkness** from the Old English *glomung*, from *glom*: twilight; *for etymology, see box below*

e.g. The number of road accidents increases during the **gloaming** because many drivers haven't yet turned their lights on

---

*gloaming is the early onset of twilight (which is the time immediately after sunset when the light is faint; **dusk** is the later, darker stage of twilight).*

*Note that the adjective to describe twilight is **crepuscular** (from the Latin crepusculum: twilight).*

---

gnomic (adj.)
= *(of an utterance)* **enigmatic and pithy** from the Greek
gnomai: sayings, maxims

e.g. 'My wallpaper and I are fighting a duel to the death.
One or other of us has to go,' was Oscar Wilde's **gnomic**
deathbed utterance

Grand Guignol (phrase)
= **drama that entertains but is horrific** *for etymology, see box below*

e.g. The most famous example of **Grand Guignol** in recent times is the film *Sweeney Todd* starring Johnny Depp

---

*The English term **Grand Guignol** originates from the name of the French theatre* Le Théâtre du Grand-Guignol *(The Theatre of the Big Puppet), which was formed in Paris in 1897.*

This theatre was a place of gore, staging horror shows; the success of each performance was gauged by the number of people who fainted.

After the all too real horrors of World War II, demand for artificial horror subsided and the theatre closed. However, we still use the word today to refer to any play or film which uses gory special effects to shock.

---

grass roots (phrase)
= **ordinary people rather than those at the centre of major political activity** *for etymology, see box opposite*

e.g. When Oliver Cromwell abolished Christmas in the 17th century and turned it into an ordinary working day, he should have predicted that the **grass roots** of his party would object to this

The term **grass roots** was first used by a certain Senator Beveridge of Indiana, who said in 1912 of the Progressive Party that had just been formed:

'This party has come from the "grass roots". It has grown from the soil of people's hard necessities.'

Today, we continue to use the phrase **grass roots** to refer to any political movement that has arisen as a result of discontent amongst ordinary voters – rather than as a result of politicians' machinations.

H

hagiography (noun)
= **a biography that idealises the person described, as if they were a saint** from the Greek *hagios*: holy, and *graphe*: writing; *hagiography literally means 'the writing of the lives of the saints'*

e.g. The book with the title of *The Rise of Boris Johnson* suggests a **hagiography** of the politican but in fact offers a balanced view of its subject

halcyon (adj.)
= **denoting a happy and peaceful time in the past** *for etymology, see box below*

e.g. Most people look back on their childhood as consisting of **halcyon** days

---

*In Greek mythology, the halcyon (**halkyon** in Greek) was a type of kingfisher that built its nest by the sea.*

To explain how any bird could bring up its young by a noisy and raging sea, the Greeks attributed to this kingfisher the power to render the wind and the waves calm.

*So it is that today, when we refer to **halcyon days**, we evoke a period of calm.*

---

hamartia (noun)
= **a flaw that brings about the destruction of a hero** *for etymology, see box below*

e.g. Marilyn Monroe's hamartia was a fondness for men in power: many say this lead to her death

---

*The term **hamartia** was first used by the ancient Greeks to describe an error in judgement.*

*Nowadays, **hamartia** is used to mean something slightly different: a character's 'tragic flaw' that ultimately destroys him.*

A good example occurs in one of the most famous novels of the 20th century: The Great Gatsby *(1925). Jay Gatsby's **hamartia** is his unreciprocated love for a married lady called Daisy; when Daisy runs over and kills a woman by accident, Gatsby claims it is he who was responsible and, as a result, is murdered by the victim's husband.*

---

harbinger (noun)
= **something that heralds the approach of another** *for etymology, see box below*

e.g. As a child, Oprah Winfrey played games interviewing the crows in her garden: this was the **harbinger** of her success as a chat show host

---

*The word **harbinger** derives from the French word **herbergier**, which means 'someone who provides lodging' (itself originating from **herberge**, meaning 'lodging'). Later the word came to mean 'a man who went ahead to find lodgings for an army' – hence 'a forerunner', and this sense persists today.*

harpy (noun)
= **a woman known for her grasping nature** *for etymology, see box below*

e.g. If an attractive young woman marries a rich old man, society is quick to label the woman a **harpy**

A **harpy** was in Greek mythology a flying creature with a woman's head but a monster's body. Harpies would descend from the sky and snatch food from the hands of humans on the ground:

It is for this reason that the literal meaning of **harpy** (**harpazein**. to snatch in Greek) is 'someone who snatches'. Today we continue to refer to any grasping woman as a **harpy**.

89

hawkish (adj.)
= **advocating war or aggression** *hawkish derives from 'hawk', a warlike bird; the direct opposite of* **dovish** *(see p. 55)*

e.g. Towards the end of his life, Elvis Presley amassed an arsenal of weapons – including 32 handguns – because chronic drug abuse had made him **hawkish**

heft (noun)
= **the amount of power that one wields** *(when used figuratively)*; **OR weight** *(when used literally) heft derives from 'heft', the obsolete past participle of the verb 'heave'*

e.g. George Bush's detractors depicted him as lacking the intellectual **heft** for the Presidency

hegemony (noun)
= **leadership** *from the Greek hegemon: leader*

e.g. With three successive league championships between 2007 and 2009, Manchester United's **hegemony** within English football is clear

heterogeneous (adj.)
= **made up of diverse units** *from the Greek heteros: other, and genos: a kind; for etymology, see box below*

e.g. Aside from a love of tennis, it is hard to find commonality among the crowds at the Wimbledon tennis championships: they form a **heterogeneous** group

---

The direct opposite of **heterogeneous** *is* **homogeneous**, *meaning 'made up of units that are exactly the same as each other'.*

For example, penguins are pretty much indistinguishable to humans: in other words, as far as we are concerned, these birds form a 'homogeneous' mass.

hew to (verb)
= **to stick to** *deriving from the 19th-century phrase 'to hew to the line', meaning 'to cut evenly with a saw'; this reconciles the German root,* hauen: *'to cut' with the seemingly contradictory English expression 'to hew to', meaning 'to stick to'*

e.g. Steven Spielberg's films – *Jaws*, for example – all **hew to** his action-packed vision of story-telling

hidebound (adj.)
= **unwilling to adapt due to one's upbringing** *for etymology, see box below*

e.g. In *Romeo and Juliet*, both sets of parents cannot accept the union of their progeny because they are **hidebound** by historical feuds with one another

*hidebound was first used in the 16th century to describe cattle that had been undernourished, which led to their skin clinging closely to their back and ribs (and in this sense, their innnards were **bound** together by their **hides** alone).*

hidebound then evolved in meaning to refer to undernourished human beings, before assuming today's usage – which is 'undernourished in outlook' and thus 'unwilling to change'.

highfalutin (adj.)
= *(of language)* **grand-sounding** *highfalutin derives from the words 'high' and 'fluting': together, these words mean 'to speak in a melodious way reminiscent of the sound of a flute'*

e.g. Novels are divided into those that are commercial, such as *The Da Vinci Code* – and those that are considered **highfalutin**, such as Proust's works

hinterland (noun)
= **a realm beyond the things that are known (about someone or something)** *from the German,* hinter: *behind, and* land: *land; hinterland literally refers to the uncharted areas beyond a river's banks*

e.g. In the two bestsellers he wrote before he became President, Barack Obama discusses his religious beliefs and other areas of his **hinterland**

hortatory (adj.)
= **vigorously encouraging** *from the Latin* hortari: *to exhort*

e.g. While conducting, Tchaikovsky held onto his chin with one hand: he had a phobia that his head would roll off otherwise due to his **hortatory** hand movements

hubris (noun)
= **excessive pride** *for etymology, see box opposite*

e.g. Bernard Madoff showed **hubris** in believing he could deceive so many investors forever; nemesis came when his fraud was discovered and he was imprisoned for life

hubris was the term given by the Greeks to describe the behaviour of anyone whose excessive pride led him or her to challenge the gods.

Excessive pride is traditionally punished by the equal and opposite force of retributive justice; the Greeks called this power **nemesis** *(see p. 131) the contemporary expression 'pride comes before a fall' also describes this relationship.*

So, such a display of **hubris** *by Bernard Madoff – who thought he could fool all of the people all of the time – was always going to be punished by* **nemesis**.

husband (verb)

= *(of resources)* **to use sparingly** from the Old Norse *hus*: a house

e.g. Oprah Winfrey was born to a single teenage mother who had to **husband** the few resources she had

Hydra
= **a problem that is hard to conquer because it will not go away** *for etymology, see box below*

e.g. Trying to stop the spread of AIDS in Africa is like trying to kill the **Hydra**: there may be short-lived successes but, sadly, the problem seems perennial

---

*The Lernaean **Hydra** was in Greek mythology a sea monster with many heads who guarded an underwater entrance to the Underworld. If one of its heads was chopped off, two would grow back in its place; but there was hope for anyone seeking to vanquish the Hydra in combat as only one of its heads was immortal.*

As one of his 12 labours, Hercules had to defeat the Hydra. He did this by chopping off each head, then by having his nephew cauterise each stump to prevent regrowth. Hercules then pushed a huge rock on top of the immortal head.

*Today, we continue to refer to a problem that seems impossible to overcome as a **Hydra**.*

---

hyperbole (noun)
= **deliberate exaggeration for effect** from the Greek *huperbole*: excess, from *huper*: above, and *ballein*: to throw

e.g. When people exclaim 'over my dead body!', they are not talking about literally dying for a cause but are using **hyperbole** to make a point

idée fixe (noun)
= **an idea that has become an obsession** from the French
idée fixe: fixed idea

e.g. Imelda Marcos accumulated as many pairs of shoes
as possible: amassing footwear was an idée fixe for her

ideologue (noun)
= **a dogmatic follower of an ideology** from the Greek *idea*:
form, and *logos*: word

e.g. Iran's status as a fundamentalist Islamic republic was
cemented by the **ideologue** Ayatollah Khomeini (1900–
1989)

idiosyncratic (adj.)
= *(of a characteristic)* **peculiar to an individual** from the
Greek *idios*: private, and *sunkratos*: mixed together

e.g. Jimmy Connors's double-handed backhand was a key
part of his **idiosyncratic** style on the tennis court

imbroglio (noun)
= **a very messy and embarassing situation** from the
Italian, *imbrogliare*: to confuse

e.g. When his wife's younger sister died, Charles Dickens
took the ring off the dead woman's finger and wore it until
he died: this caused quite an **imbroglio**

immanent (adj.)
= **existing in** from the Latin *in-*: in, and *manere*: to remain

e.g. While we are all aware that death is **immanent** in life,
we still find it hard to accept the thought of our own
mortality

impassible (adj.)
= **incapable of feeling hardship** from the Latin *in*: not, and
pass-: suffered (from the verb, *pati*)

e.g. Indian fakirs who walk barefoot across hot coals give
the impression of being **impassible**

impecunious (adj.)

= **poor** from the Latin *im-*: not, and *pecunia*: money; *impecunious literally means 'having no money'*

e.g. Audrey Hepburn's grave is a small mound marked by a simple cross – to look at it, you might assume the actress was **impecunious**

impervious (adj.)

= **not affected by** from the Latin *im-*: no, and *pervius*: having a passage through; *impervious literally means 'not allowing fluid to pass through'*

e.g. From the age of eight, Mark Twain smoked on average 30 cigars a day until he died: he was **impervious** to doctors' advice to quit

imprimatur (noun)

= **a person's guarantee that something is of good quality** *for etymology, see box below*

e.g. Kim Jong-il's youngest son, Kim Jong-un, is expected to assume control of North Korea on his father's death because he enjoys his father's **imprimatur**

---

imprimatur means in Latin, 'let it be printed'.

Imprimatur at first described an official declaration by the Roman Catholic Church that a book contained no errors in matters of Catholic doctrine – and so could be read by the faithful.

*The word **imprimatur** today has a wider meaning, referring to a guarantee by anyone that something is up to scratch.*

---

incandescent (adj.)
= **burning with anger; OR of blindingly good quality** from the Latin *incandescere*: to glow; *incandescent literally means 'emitting light as a result of being heated'*

e.g. Isaac Newton was so absent-minded he once used his fiancée's finger to push down the tobacco in his pipe: this made her **incandescent**

incendiary (adj.)
= **tending to stir up trouble** from the Latin *incendere*: to set fire to; *incendiary literally means 'causing fires'*

e.g. Jeremy Paxman has made **incendiary** comments about the deteriorating quality of Marks & Spencer's Y-fronts

inchoate (adj.)
= **just started and thus not in a final state** from the Latin *incohare*: to begin

e.g. Monica Lewinksy must wonder what might have been had Bill Clinton not called off their affair when it was still **inchoate**

incongruous (adj.)
= **not in harmony with the other elements of something** from the Latin *incongruus*, from *in-*: not, and *congruus*: agreeing

e.g. When Charlie Chaplin was 54, he married an 18-year-old girl; this age difference made the couple look **incongruous**

indentured (adj.)

= *(of a labourer)* **bound by a formal agreement** from the Latin *in-*: into, and *dens, dent-*: a tooth; an indenture originally referred to a document that was indented; then to a sealed agreement binding an apprentice to his master

e.g. Some women form such close bonds with their mothers that they seem **indentured** to them

indigent (adj.)

= **impoverished** from the Latin *indigere*: to need

e.g. As a noted philanthropist, billionaire stock market trader George Soros donates money to the **indigent**

ineffable (adj.)

= *(of a sentiment)* **too great to be uttered in words** from the Latin *ineffabilis*: from *in-*: not, and *effabilis*, from *effari*: to utter

e.g. When they attend church, religious people speak of experiencing **ineffable** joy

ineluctable (adj.)

= **inescapable** from the Latin *in-*: not, and *eluctari*: to struggle out

e.g. After Lehman Brothers collapsed, a worldwide financial crisis became **ineluctable**

in extremis (phrase)

= **in a very troublesome situation** from the Latin *in extremis*: in the outermost parts

e.g. When the sailors were 50 miles from shore, a storm suddenly arose and they found themselves **in extremis**

infelicity (noun)
= **an unpleasing manner of expression; OR unhappiness**
from the Latin *infelix*: unhappy

e.g. The speech of young children who are still learning how to talk is littered with **infelicities**

infraction (noun)
= **a breaking of a rule** from the Latin *infractio*: a breaking, from *infringere*, from *in-*: into, and *frangere*: to break

e.g. If any player other than the goalkeeper uses his hands on a football pitch, he is guilty of an **infraction** of the rules

inquisitorial (adj.)
= **so prying as to be insulting** from the Latin *inquirere*: to inquire; *inquisitorial literally means '(of a trial) in which the judge has as role of inquirer'*

e.g. Many people associate the concept of psychotherapy with lying on a couch whilst an **inquisitorial** individual asks about your childhood

insignia (noun)
= **a mark that characterises something** from the Latin *insignis*: distinguished as if by a mark

e.g. Instead of buying a ring, the film producer Matthew Vaughn presented Claudia Schiffer with a tortoise as an **insignia** of their engagement

insouciance (noun)
= **an attitude devoid of worry** from the French *insouciant*: not caring, from *in-*: not, and *souciant*: worrying

e.g. Princess Grace's fatal car crash was on a road she knew well from filming *To Catch a Thief*: no, it was not **insouciance** that killed the actress but a stroke

insurrection (noun)
= **the act of rising up against an authority** from the Latin *insurrectio*, from *insurgere*: to rise up

e.g. Actor Toby Stephens has joked he will never play James Bond because casting a Bond 'with reddish hair would cause **insurrection**'

internecine (adj.)
= **relating to strife within a group of people** from the Latin *inter-*: among, and *necare*: to kill

e.g. The novelist Marcel Proust enjoyed placing starving rats in the same cage; when they tore each other to pieces, he would become sexually excited by this **internecine** display

interregnum (noun)
= **the period falling between reigns by two different rulers** from the Latin *inter-*: between, and *regnum*: reign

e.g. The gap between the Queen's death and the coronation of her successor will form an **interregnum**

invective (noun)
= **abusive language** from the Latin *invectivus*: abusive, from *invectus*, past participle of *invehere*: to attack with words

e.g. Tired of his wife's **invective**, *War and Peace* author Leo Tolstoy left her a note stating his wish to spend his 'last days alone and in silence'. He died soon after

inveigh against (verb)
= **to verbally attack (something)** from the Latin *invehi*: to attack with words

e.g. Knowing that the public blames capitalists for the credit crunch, politicians frequently **inveigh against** bankers

invidious (adj.)
= *(of a comparison)* **discriminating between people in an unfair fashion** from the Latin *invidia*: envy; *invidious literally means 'arousing envy in others'*

e.g. A mother will rarely say which of her sons is her favourite because she knows no happiness can come from such an **invidious** comment

inviolable (adj.)
= **never to be destroyed** from the Latin *inviolabilis*: invulnerable, from *in-*: not, and *violare*: to do violence to

e.g. The Catholic Church does not allow divorcées to marry again, viewing marriage vows as **inviolable**

irascible (adj.)
= *(of a person)* **growing angry easily** from the Latin *irasci*: to grow angry

e.g. Composer Brahms used to shoot cats with a bow and arrow: he hated them so much that the mere sight of a feline made him **irascible**

jejune (adj.)

= **too simple; OR dull** from the Latin *jejunus*: fasting; *this sense of 'being physically undernourished' (as a result of fasting) evolved to mean 'being intellectually undernourished'*

e.g. Whereas the views of most teenagers are **jejune**, the narrator of *The Catcher in the Rye* delivers mature insights that expose the hypocrisies of adults

jeremiad (noun)

= **a long moan** *for etymology, see box below*

e.g. Lord Byron was so fat he used to play cricket wearing a total of seven waistcoats in a bid to lose weight; when this failed, he embarked on a **jeremiad**

---

jeremiad derives from the name of Jeremiah, who features in the Bible.

Jeremiah was notorious for moaning – mainly about the destruction of Jerusalem (as described in The Lamentations of Jeremiah *in the Old Testament).*

Today, when we use the word **jeremiad***, we conjure up the image of one long complaint.*

journeyman (noun)
= **a worker or sportsman who is reliable but not the best**
for etymology, see box below

e.g. Roger Federer is famous but few people know the
names of the lower-ranked **journeymen** of the tennis
world

*In Middle English, 'a journey' used to mean 'a day's work'
and a **journeyman** therefore referred to a worker who was
paid for each day he worked – but whom the employer did
not consider good enough to give a full-time contract to.*

*When we use the word **journeyman** today, we evoke this
perjorative sense of someone who is an 'also-ran'.*

juju (noun)
= **a lucky charm** from the French *joujou*: toy

e.g. James Joyce was a superstitious man who used to carry around rabbits' ears and other **jujus** to bring himself luck

juvenilia

juvenilia (noun)
= **works produced by an artist in his youth** from the Latin
juvenis: a young person

e.g. Imagine the excitement if somebody discovered the
unread **juvenilia** of Shakespeare

Kafkaesque (adj.)

= *(of a situation)* **marked by menace and complexity** *for etymology, see box overleaf*

e.g. Britons who are put on trial abroad often find the process **Kafkaesque** compared to the relatively straightforward British legal system

ken

Kafkaesque refers to those unpleasant situations and ideas that are suggestive of the books of Czech novelist Franz Kafka (1883–1924).

Kafka's most famous novel, The Trial, tells the story of a man arrested and prosecuted by an enigmatic authority; but he never finds out what he has done wrong.

The term 'Kafkaesque' is today applied to any situation where an individual is accused of a crime but where little – if any – evidence is offered to substantiate the accusation.

ken (noun)
= **the range of what one knows** from the German *kennen*: to know

e.g. Ivan the Terrible (1530–1584) used to sew victims into bearskins, then hunt them down with hounds; such cruelty is beyond most people's **ken**

L

lackadaisical (adj.)
= **lacking in keenness** *from the archaic interjection 'lack-a-day' of a listless person which was used to convey disapproval; a phrase*

e.g. John Wayne made acting look natural because he appeared **lackadaisical** on screen

laconic (adj.)
= **uttering few words** *for etymology, see box below*

e.g. Boxer Mike Tyson never gave much away in post-fight interviews: he is a **laconic** man

---

laconic originates from a place in Greece called 'Laconia' (to which the Greeks gave the adjective Lakonikos*).*

The inhabitants of Laconia (which was also known as Sparta) were notorious for not saying much; hence, when we call someone **laconic** *today, we evoke this sense of terseness.*

---

lacuna (noun)
= **a gap that has not been filled** *from the Latin lacuna: a pond*

e.g. After she read of a friend's death, Florence Nightingale was so affected by the resulting **lacuna** in her life that she cancelled her daily newspaper lest she read of any other such deaths

lambent (adj.)

= *(of light)* **flickering softly;** *(of humour)* **brilliant but with a light touch** from the Latin *lambent-*: licking, from *lambere*: to lick

e.g. 'I told you I was ill' were the words chosen by Spike Milligan for his epitaph: it was typical of him to treat his own death with such a **lambent** wit

lampoon (verb)

= **to hold up to public ridicule** from the French *lampoon*: originally meaning 'a drinking song', later 'a lampoon', deriving from *lampons*: let us drink, a refrain of 17th-century songs

e.g. For years, the magazine *Private Eye* has **lampooned** celebrities

lapidary (adj.)

= *(of language)* **so elegant that it is worth engraving on stone** from the Latin *lapis, lapidis*: a stone

e.g. Ernest Hemingway's dislike of adjectives means his sentences are concise and **lapidary**

lard with (verb)

= **to enliven (sentences) with a variety of expressions** from the Greek *larinos*: fat; *lard with literally means 'to smear a foodstuff with lard to prevent it from drying out during storage'*

e.g. Ex-French President Mitterrand was fond of **larding** his speeches with quotations from Balzac and other French writers of old

leaven (verb)
= **to change (something) for the better** from the Latin *levare*: to lift

e.g. The director Quentin Tarantino uses humorous dialogue to **leaven** the violence in his films

legerdemain (noun)
= **sleight of hand** from the French *leger de main*: light of hand; *legerdemain literally means 'skilful use of one's hand when performing conjuring tricks'*

e.g. For years Oscar Wilde exercised considerable **legerdemain** in concealing his homosexuality from the public; but eventually he was outed and jailed

leonine (adj.)
= **like a lion** from the Latin *leo, leonis*: a lion

e.g. Bjorn Borg has maintained his long yellow hair into his middle age and with it his **leonine** look

lese-majesty (noun)
= **an attack on authority** from the Latin *laesa majestas*: injured sovereignty; *lese-majesty literally means 'the insulting of a ruler'*

e.g. The French revolution (1789–1799), and the use of the guillotine that accompanied it, was the ultimate act of **lese-majesty**

leviathan (noun)
= something very large, especially a large sea creature
for etymology, see box below

e.g. Billionaires often buy themselves large yachts and then hold parties on these **leviathans**

---

leviathan is used in the Bible to refer to various monsters, such as the whale and the crocodile (in Job*) and to the ultimate monster, the Devil (in* Isaiah*).*

Today, it continues to evoke any dangerous aquatic creature – often a whale but not always – or any large organisation or object (not necessarily a sea creature.)

---

libertine (noun)
= a person, especially a man, who disregards all moral codes, particularly in sexual matters from the Latin *libertinus*: freedman, from *liber*: free

e.g. In the film *Dangerous Liaisons*, John Malkovich plays the ultimate **libertine**: an aristocrat who sexually corrupts the innocent

licentious (adj.)
= unbridled in sexual matters from the Latin *licentia*: freedom

e.g. James Bond beds several women in each film, reflecting his **licentious** approach to relationships

Lilliputian (adj.)

= **very small in size; OR trivial** *for etymology, see box below*

e.g. Paris may be the capital city of France, but it seems **Lilliputian** when compared to the sprawling metropolis that is London

---

*The **Lilliputians** were people around six inches tall who inhabited the fictional island of Lilliput in Jonathan Swift's novel* Gulliver's Travels *(1726). In the novel, Gulliver is washed up on the island of Lilliput, and implored by the tiny Lilliputians to fight the people on a neighbouring island.*

The island of Lilliput was used by Swift to parody England at the time. For example, Swift talks about a conflict in Lilliput between those people who prefer to open an egg from its big end and those people who opt for the small end; this is a reference to the ongoing arguments in England between the Catholics (the 'Big-Endians') and the Protestants (the 'Little-Endians').

*Today, we use the word **Lilliputian** to denote something that is physically tiny or a matter that is very trivial.*

---

liminal (adj.)

= **in a transitional state** from the Latin *limen, liminis*: a threshold; *liminal* literally means 'standing on both sides of a threshold'

e.g. As he waited for the defeated President Bush to see out his final days in office, President-elect Barack Obama found himself in a **liminal** state

limpid (adj.)
= *(of liquid or of writing)* **crystal clear** from the Latin *limpidus*: clear

e.g. Brigitte Bardot was an iconic sex symbol of the 1960s, renowned for her **limpid** blue eyes

lingua franca (phrase)
= **a language that is taken on as a common language between speakers whose mother tongues are different** from the Italian, *lingua franca*: Frankish tongue

e.g. English people on holiday in France use 'franglais' to communicate with the locals: basic exchanges can be effected using this **lingua franca**

litotes (noun)
= **ironic understatement in which a sentiment is expressed by negating its contrary proposition** from the Greek *litotes*, from *litos*: plain, meagre

e.g. I deduced from my English teacher's use of the **litotes**: 'I am not unfamiliar with the works of Dickens', that he was an expert on the novelist

lodestar (noun)
= **a person or thing that serves as a guiding force** from the Middle English *lodesterre*, from *lode*: way, and *steere*: star; *lodestar literally means 'a star that is used to guide the course of a ship'*

e.g. Barack Obama cites Martin Luther King so often that it is clear King is a **lodestar** for him

logorrheic (adj.)
= **uncontrollably talkative** from the Greek *logos*: word, and *rhien*: to flow

e.g. Freud said of the Irish: "This is one race of people whom psychoanalysis is of no use whatsoever." Presumably because the Irish are so logorrheic that it is hard to know which bits coming out of their mouths are important.

lore (noun)
= **a body of knowledge on a topic, that has typically been passed from person to person via the oral tradition** from the Old English *lar*: instruction, of Germanic origin, related to the German *Lehre*: learning

e.g. When writing the Bond novel *Devil May Care*, Sebastian Faulks consulted Ian Fleming's family on matters of Bond **lore**

Luddite

Luddite (noun)
= **a person who is against new technology** *for etymology, see box opposite*

e.g. Some people over the age of 70 are **Luddites** who do not know how to surf the Internet

Luddite derives from the name of Ned Lud, a member of a 19th-century group of English cotton mill workers who destroyed machinery that was threatening to take over their jobs.

*Today, when we call someone a **Luddite**, we are referring to someone who opposes new technology of any kind.*

ludic (adj.)
= **playful** from the Latin *ludere*: to play

e.g. Playwright Arthur Miller praised his ex-wife Marilyn Monroe for her sense of fun, and noted that most adults lacked this **ludic** quality

Machiavellian (adj.)

= **wily and unscrupulous in furthering one's own career**
for etymology, see box below

e.g. The public regards politicians as **Machiavellian** types

---

Machiavellian originates from the name of Machiavelli, a Renaissance Italian statesman.

Machiavelli's book **The Prince** *(1532) advises rulers that unethical methods are necessary if power is to be seized and effectively wielded.*

Today, we continue to describe someone as **Machiavellian** *if they stab rivals in the back, or mistreat people in other ways in the pursuit of power.*

---

magisterial (adj.)

= **authoritative** from the Latin *magister*: master

e.g. Steven Spielberg's self-confidence means he exudes a **magisterial** air on set

malapropism (noun)
= **mistakenly using one word in the place of another (often with an unintentionally comic effect)** *for etymology, see box opposite*

e.g. I decided to tell my friends about my *flamenco* dancing lessons but it came out wrong and I ended up saying: 'I can dance a *flamingo* now'; they laughed at my **malapropism**

malaproprism derives from the name of the character Mrs Malaprop in Richard Sheridan's play The Rivals (1775).

Mrs Malaprop has a habit of getting words confused, which is a source of humour in the play. Her name was chosen because of the link to the French phrase mal à propos, *which means 'ill-suited' and describes perfectly the jumbled order of her words.*

Today, when we say that someone has committed a **malapropism***, we mean they are guilty of a similar linguistic slip-up.*

malfeasance (noun)
= **malpractice, especially by a public official** from the Old French *mal*: evil, and *faisance*: activity

e.g. The MPs' expenses' scandal revealed that politicians had been using taxpayers' money to pay a variety of items for personal use: this **malfeasance** caused a public outcry

malinger (verb)
= **to pretend to be ill to avoid work** from the Old French *mal*: wrongly, and *haingre*: weak

e.g. Every year the government loses millions of pounds owing to workers pretending to be sick; as taxpayers, we are all victims of this **malingering**

mandarin (noun)
= **a powerful government worker** ultimately deriving from the Sanskrit *mantri*: a counsellor; a *mandarin literally refers to a bureaucrat in imperial China (AD 900–1800)*

e.g. In the UK, the head of MI6 is one of the most powerful **mandarins**

Manichaean (adj.)
= relating to a view that divides the world very starkly into good and evil *for etymology, see box below*

e.g. George Bush spoke about certain countries forming an 'axis of evil': this implies he sees the world in **Manichaean** terms, with the USA being 'good' and these other mentioned countries being 'evil'

Manichaean derives from 'Manichaeism', a 3rd-century religion that was one of the most popular in the world at the time.

This religion was based on the teachings of the Iranian prophet Mani who was privy to divine truths from a spirit who visited him.

*Manichaeism is distinguished by its viewing the world as a clear-cut struggle between good (or 'spirituality') and evil (or 'materialism'); today, when we call someone **Manichaean**, we mean they see the world as being divided very clearly between good and evil.*

---

manqué (adj.)
= referring to someone who missed out on a particular role from the French *manquer*: to miss

e.g. US senator Ted Kennedy never achieved his political potential because allegations of drinking and womanising dogged him throughout his life: he was the President **manqué**

marionette (noun)
= a puppet controlled from above by strings attached to it from the French *marionette*: little Mary, the diminutive form of *Marion*, which is itself the diminutive of *Marie*

e.g. The SS was a major Nazi organisation composed of one million of Hitler's **marionettes**

marmoreal (adj.)
= **like marble** from the Latin *marmor*: marble

e.g. To those who found actress Grace Kelly **marmoreal**, Alfred Hitchcock said of his leading lady that she had 'fire under the ice'

martinet (noun)
= **a strict taskmaster** *for etymology, see box below*

e.g. 'Fat farms' are populated by obese people who are whipped into shape by **martinets**

---

martinet derives from the name of the 17th-century Frenchman Jean Martinet, a highly-ordered man who trained soldiers.

Tired of having to deal with fickle mercenaries, Martinet devised a rigorous programme to turn members of the public into effective military servicemen.

*It is a cruel irony that this paragon of discipline was killed by 'friendly fire': a fatal form of ill-discipline. Today, the word **martinet** refers to any disciplinarian.*

---

maunder on (verb)
= **to talk in a meandering fashion; OR to move or act as if time is of no concern** from the Old English *maund*: to beg, deriving from the French *mendier*: to beg

e.g. In his satirical sketches of political figures, Rory Bremner contorts his face to better depict his victims as he **maunders on** in their tone of voice

maw (noun)
= **the throat of a ravenous animal** from the German *Magen*: stomach

e.g. *The Hound of the Baskervilles* is a story about a giant dog suspected of killing people using its fearsome **maw**

mawkish (adj.)
= **sentimental in a nausea-inducing way** from the Old English *mawke*: maggot; *mawkish originally meant 'to be disgusted', as if by putrid meat*

e.g. The final scene of a 'rom com' typically involves a girl running into the arms of a boy or some other equally **mawkish** scene

mellifluous (adj.)
= *(of a voice)* **honey-coated** from the Latin *mellifluus*, from *mel*: honey, and *fluere*: to flow

e.g. The advent of sound meant Clark Gable's career took off overnight because there was suddenly huge demand for his **mellifluous** voice

menagerie (noun)
= **a diverse mixture of people or animals** *for etymology, see box opposite*

e.g. Each year the cast of *Celebrity Big Brother* is made up of a variety of people in the public eye, such as TV stars and glamour models: a veritable **menagerie** of individuals

A **menagerie** was a 16th-century French term used to describe a collection of exotic animals kept in captivity; the French word ménagerie is derived from the word ménage, meaning 'a household'.

A **menagerie** was often retained by a royal court, not so much as to study the animal world but rather to signify the opulence of the menagerie's owner (as exotic animals were very expensive to purchase).

Today, **menagerie** refers to any diverse collection of things or people.

mercurial (adj.)
= **very moody** *for etymology, see box below*

e.g. Idi Amin (1925–2003), the despotic ruler of Uganda for many years, was a **mercurial** man who had people executed on a whim

---

mercurial derives from the Latin word mercurialis, *which meant 'relating to the god Mercury'.*

The god Mercury would fly quickly from one place to another and back again – it is this erraticism (albeit of a mental, rather than a physical, kind) that we evoke when we call someone **mercurial** *today.*

---

meretricious (adj.)
= **alluring but vulgar** *from the Latin meretrix, meretricis: a prostitute;* *meretricious* *literally means 'like a prostitute'*

e.g. A woman who has obviously had breast augmentation surgery holds a **meretricious** appeal for some men

metonym (noun)
= **a word used instead of another word with which it is closely linked** *from the Greek metonomasia: change of name*

e.g. Newspapers are produced using a printing press; hence the term 'the press' has become a **metonym** to describe all newspapers collectively

miasma (noun)
= **an atmosphere that has been polluted** from the Greek *miama*: a stain (especially due to a murder)

e.g. During the Second World War, Jews in Germany lived their lives in a **miasma** of fear and suspicion

microcosm (noun)
= **a situation that reflects on a smaller scale the qualities of a larger situation** from the Greek *micros*: little, and *kosmos*: world

e.g. Some saw England's defeat of Germany in the 1966 Football World Cup as a **microcosm** of England's defeat of Germany in World War II

mimesis (noun)
= **the rendering of the real world in art** from the Greek *mimeisthai*: to imitate

e.g. Shakespeare's play *Henry V* is a mimesis of Britain's victory over the French at Agincourt

misnomer (noun)
= **a name that is wrong** from the Old French *mesnommer*: to misname, from *mes-*: wrongly, and *nommer*: to name

e.g. A horseshoe crab looks more like a stingray than a crab: so the term 'horseshoe *crab*' is a **misnomer**

monoglot (adj.)
= **speaking one language only** from the Greek *monos*: single, and *glotta*: tongue

e.g. As English is spoken the world over, most English people get away with being **monoglot**

monolithic (adj.)

= *(of an organisation or a building)* **very large and without quirks** from the Greek *monos*: single, and *lithos*: stone; *monolithic literally means 'formed of a single large block of stone'*

e.g. The Chinese Communist Party plays down the importance of any one individual, reflecting its **monolithic** nature

moratorium (noun)

= **a temporary ban of an activity** from the Latin *moratorius*: delaying

e.g. With the world's supply of fish on the wane, governments agreed a **moratorium** on cod fishing

mordant (adj.)

= *(of humour)* **biting** from the French *mordre*: to bite

e.g. The comments directed by Simon Cowell towards aspirant singers on his TV show *The X Factor* are full of **mordant** humour

multifarious (adj.)

= **having many parts** from the Latin *multifarious*: manifold, combined with the Greek *farius*: showing

e.g. Catholicism and Anglicanism are two of the **multifarious** branches of the Christian faith

munificent (adj.)

= **particularly generous** from the Latin *munificus*: bountiful e.g. Robert Redford used his salary from *Butch Cassidy and the Sundance Kid* to set up the Sundance Film Festival for independent films: a **munificent** gesture

myopic (adj.)
= **having no foresight** from the Greek *muops*: nearsighted, from *muein*: to close the eyes, and *ops*: eye; *myopic literally means 'shortsighted'*

e.g. Mike Tyson disconcerted Evander Holyfield by taking a bite out of his ear during their boxing fight; later, though, Tyson was disqualified, proving this was a **myopic** tactic

nativism (noun)
= **the policy of favouring the interests of native-born inhabitants above those of immigrants** deriving from the English word, *native*

e.g. There is a campaign on Facebook called 'People United Against Nativism' whose slogan is: '**nativism** is *so* 19th century'

nebulous / amorphous (adj.)
= *(of a shape)* **unclear** *nebulous* derives from the Latin nebula: a cloud (*nebulous* literally means 'in the form of a cloud'); *amorphous* derives from the Greek amorphous: shapeless, from a-: without, and morphe: form

e.g. Jamie Oliver has never been filmed cooking in the nude, so the reasons for his being called *The Naked Chef* are **nebulous / amorphous**

nemesis (noun)
= **the punishment for excessive pride** *(see also **hubris**)* from the Greek *nemesis*: retribution

e.g. Bernard Madoff showed hubris in believing he could deceive so many investors forever; **nemesis** came when his fraud was discovered he was imprisoned for life

neologism (noun)
= **a newly invented word or expression** from the Greek *neos*: new, and *logos*: word

e.g. The advent of the Internet led to **neologisms** such as 'to surf the net' which are now commonly used

netherworld (noun)
= **the part of society involved in crime** from the Old English *nether*: lower, and *world*; *netherworld literally means: 'the underworld of the dead'*

e.g. Newspapers often report murders and other crimes; it seems that every type of **netherworld** is of interest to journalists

nexus (noun)
= **a connection binding together two or more things** from the Latin *nex-*: bound, from *nectere*: to bind

e.g. Barack Obama has declared his intention to break the **nexus** between 'Big Oil' and politics

nimbus (noun)
= **a large rain cloud** from the Latin *nimbus*: cloud

e.g. I rushed home to grab an umbrella after I saw the **nimbuses** overhead

noblesse oblige (phrase)
= **the responsibility of privileged people to show generosity to those less privileged** *for etymology, see box below*

e.g. Angelina Jolie does much charity work for landmine victims: she is a celebrity who exercises **noblesse oblige**

In his novel Le Lys dans la vallée *(which translates as* The Lily of the Valley*), the 19th century French novelist Balzac summarises his advice to a rich young man by the two words:* 'noblesse oblige!'

This phrase – which literally means 'nobility creates obligations' – is cited today as a reminder that, with great wealth comes great responsibility: the rich have a duty to help the poor.

*Today, we use the phrase **noblesse oblige** to remind someone who has enjoyed success that they should help others who have fared less well.*

nomenclature (noun)
= **the act of choosing names for things; OR the collection of names thus chosen** from the Latin *nomenclatura*, from *nomen*: name, and *clatura*: calling (from *calare*: to call)

e.g. To describe female acting professionals, the term 'actors' is now preferred to the original **nomenclature** of 'actresses'

normative (adj.)
= **establishing a rule of behaviour** from the Latin *norma*: a rule

e.g. Marriage has a **normative** effect on society because it ensures communities are composed of tight-knit groups made up of parents and offspring

nostrum (noun)
= **a favourite but usually hopeless scheme for effecting social improvement** from the Latin *nostrum*: 'our own make' – a term used in ancient times by quacks claiming special virtue for their own make of wares; *a nostrum literally means 'an ineffective medicine prepared by an unqualified person'*

e.g. To stem rising numbers of single parent families and encourage more family units, John Major announced his **nostrum**: the *Back to Basics* campaign

numinous (adj.)
= **relating to the spiritual and the mysterious** from the
Latin *numen, numis*: divine power

e.g. In the secular 21st century, art and literature have for
many replaced religion as a means of accessing the
numinous

obfuscate (verb)

= **to bewilder** from the Latin *obfuscare*: to darken;
obfuscate literally means 'to make obscure'

e.g. Literary novels sometimes fail to sell well because the
average reader finds the complicated structure of such
novels frequently **obfuscates** the story (if indeed there is
one)

oblique (adj.)
= **not direct in dealing with a point** from the Latin
obliquus: slanted; *oblique literally means 'neither parallel nor
at a right angle to a specified line'*

e.g. Jeremy Paxman once asked Michael Howard exactly
the same question 12 times in a row because he was
finding the politician's responses so **oblique**

obscurantist (adj.)
= **describes someone who casts a veil over the facts**
from the Latin *obscurare*: to make dark

e.g. After a long period of being **obscurantist** on their
interrogation methods, the CIA finally admitted it had
used 'water-boarding' on terrorist suspects

obtuse (adj.)
= **annoyingly slow to grasp (something)** from the Latin
obtusus, past participle of *obtundere*: to beat against

e.g. Doctors must not allow themselves to be overly
affected by human suffering: perhaps this is why they can
appear **obtuse** to some patients

oleaginous (adj.) / unctuous (adj.)
= **obsequious** *oleaginous derives from* oleaginus: *of the olive
tree, from* oleum: *oil (oleaginous literally means 'oily');
unctuous derives from the Latin* unguere: *to anoint*

e.g. Tony Blair's friends describe him as charming, while
his enemies call him **oleaginous / unctuous**

olfactory (adj.)
= **relating to the sense of smell** from the Latin *olfacere*: to
smell

e.g. To smell a bunch of flowers is an **olfactory** treat

opaque (adj.)
= **hard to make out** from the Latin *opacus*: darkened

e.g. Isaac Newton used to deliver lecture after lecture to empty rooms: his pupils had all stopped turning up because they found his talks so **opaque**

opprobrium (noun)
= **bitter criticism** from the Latin *opprobrium*: reproach, from *ob-*: against, and *probum*: disgraceful act

e.g. Homophobia attracts **opprobrium** in the West

ordure (noun)
= **something horrid** from the Latin *horridus*: horrid; *ordure literally means 'excrement'*

e.g. Agatha Christie hated her fictional creation Hercule Poirot, calling him 'an egocentric creep' and referring to him as though he were **ordure**

ornery (adj.)
= **ill-tempered** *ornery is a 19th-century dialectal variant of 'ordinary'*

e.g. Despite having a painful back which necessitated frequent operations, John F. Kennedy never appeared **ornery** in public

orotund (adj.)
= *(of a voice)* **full; OR** *(of writing)* **pompous** from the Latin *ore rotundo*: with rounded mouth

e.g. Actor Laurence Olivier's voice used to fill any theatre: it was one of the most **orotund** in the business

Orwellian (adj.)

= *(of an authority)* **contrary to the welfare of a free society – as described by the novelist George Orwell** *for etymology, see box below*

e.g. Belgian citizens are required to carry a national ID card at all times – an imposition which some describe as **Orwellian**

Orwellian means reminiscent of the works of George Orwell (1903–1950), particularly his novel Nineteen Eighty-Four.

In Nineteen Eighty-Four, *a civil servant called Winston Smith has the job of falsifying records to make it appear the government is always right.*

The term **Orwellian** *is today used to describe any attempt by government to control individuals by similarly-doctored propaganda or by any other means, such as surveillance.*

---

outré (adj.)

= **beyond the pale** from the French *outré*: exceeded, from the past participle of *outrer*: to exceed

e.g. Outré comments by Jonathan Ross led to his suspension without pay by the BBC for 12 weeks in 2008

oxymoron (noun)

= **a phrase involving contradictory terms placed side by side to produce an amusing effect** from the Greek *oxumoros*: pointedly foolish, from *oxus*: sharp, and *moros*: foolish

e.g. Robin Hood stole from the rich but gave to the poor: you could call him 'an honest rogue' if you like that **oxymoron**

palimpsest (noun)

= **something that displays its past (as well as its present)** *for etymology, see box below*

e.g. The police shone infrared lights inside Fred West's home, revealing **palimpsests** of bloodstains that the serial killer had sought to wash away

---

palimpsest literally refers to an ancient Roman manuscript on which the original writing had been rubbed away to make room for later writing (as was the Roman custom); hence the Greek etymology, palin: 'again', and psestos: 'scraped' – so *palimpsest* literally means 'scraped (clean and used) again'.

However the original writing was not lost forever: with the passing of time, the faint outlines of the earlier writing would reappear with sufficient clarity for scholars to read it.

Today, we use *palimpsest* to describe an object that displays its past (as well as its present) – for example, our brain is the ultimate *palimpsest*, retaining so much information about our past while also accounting for our present behaviour.

---

palliative (noun)

= **relieving a problem without curing it** from the Latin *palliatus*: cloaked

e.g. It is said that Queen Victoria used marijuana to relieve menstrual pain: the drug was her **palliative** of choice

panache (noun)
= a flamboyant conviction in one's own sense of style
from the French *panache*, itself deriving from the Italian *pennachio*: a plume of feathers

e.g. The quality that makes Roger Federer so easy to watch as a tennis player is not his fitness or serve but his overall **panache**

Panglossian (adj.)
= a person who is optimistic whatever happens *for etymology, see box below*

e.g. The press depicted Gordon Brown as **Panglossian** in taking so long to acknowledge the UK was in the grip of a credit crunch

---

Pangloss is a character in the novel Candide *by French writer Voltaire (1694-1778). He is a tutor charged with educating the young Candide, who lives in beautiful surrounds; Pangloss is an optimistic teacher whose mantra is as follows: 'all is for the best in the best possible of worlds'.*

Candide eventually leaves his pampered existence and witnesses such suffering in the world that he abandons Pangloss's rosy worldview in favour of his own pragmatic philosophy, which is: 'all you can do is tend your own garden'.

Today, we continue to describe anyone who is excessively optimistic as **Panglossian**.

---

panoply (noun)
= **an admirable collection of things** from the Latin *panoplia*: full armour, from the Greek *panoplia*: all, and *hopla*: arms

e.g. Actress Marlene Dietrich once wore a gown containing feathers from 300 swans: a **panoply** of plumage

pantheon (noun)
= **a group of illustrious people** *for etymology, see box below*

e.g. Alfred Hitchcock never received an Oscar despite his undisputed place amongst the **pantheon** of film directors

---

pantheon literally meant in ancient Greece 'a temple of all gods', deriving from the Greek words pan: *all, and* theos: *god.*

Indeed the most famous such structure retains the word in its name: the Pantheon of Rome (built in 27 BC).

Since the 16th century the word **pantheon** *has come to mean 'an exalted set of people'.*

---

paradigm (noun)
= **a model** from the Greek *paradeigma*: a model

e.g. Audrey Hepburn was the **paradigm** of success at a young age, winning an Oscar for her very first film, *Roman Holiday*

paragon (noun)
= **a person or thing viewed as a benchmark for others** *for etymology, see box below*

e.g. Cristiano Ronaldo is one of the world's most expensive players because he is a **paragon** of footballing excellence

---

paragon derives from the Italian word paragone, *meaning 'a touchstone to test gold'.*

The touchstone in question was black quartz (a semi-precious mineral), which was used for testing the quality of gold alloys by rubbing them on it and then comparing the streak left behind by the gold alloy with a streak left by pure gold (which leaves a clear yellow line behind).

Gradually **paragon** *assumed its current figurative usage, referring today to a model of excellence by which other people or things must be judged.*

(See also **touchstone***, which has a near-identical meaning.)*

---

parenthetical (adj.)
= **within (or** *as if* **within) a parenthesis, which is an explanatory phrase enclosed by curved brackets** from the Greek *parentithenai*: to put in beside

e.g. Conversations with Fidel Castro are reported to last for hours; presumably this is because the Cuban leader indulges in **parenthetical** asides when he talks

par excellence (phrase)
= **superior to others of the same kind** from the French *par excellence*: by excellence

e.g. American financier Warren Buffett has won a reputation for being an investor **par excellence**

parlay (something) into (something more valuable) (verb)
= **to convert (something) into (something more valuable)** from the Latin *par*: equal

e.g. The young Sir James Goldsmith joined his brother in a pharmaceutical venture; from this he amassed a tidy sum which he went on to **parlay into** billions

parlous (adj.)
= **fraught with danger** *parlous is a Middle English contraction of 'perilous'*

e.g. Gangster Al Capone's health was always in a **parlous** state due to his refusal to receive injections

parochial (adj.)
= **having a narrow world-view** from the Greek *paroikos*: a neighbour

e.g. The British regard Americans as having a **parochial** world-view because less than one third of Americans have passports

paroxysm (noun)
= **a sudden expression of an emotion; OR a sudden bout of a disease** from the Greek *paroxusmos*: a severe fit of a disease, deriving from *para-* (intensifying prefix) and *oxunein*: to sharpen

e.g. After his wife died in a plane crash, actor Clark Gable turned to drink in a **paroxysm** of grief

parse (verb)
= **to examine (something) closely, especially by breaking it up into parts** from the Latin *pars*: part

e.g. Scientists can easily **parse** the behaviour of chimpanzees into the conventional categories of human comportment

parsimonious (adj.)
= **frugal** from the Latin *parsimonia*: frugality

e.g. Most of the world's religions advise the faithful to lead a **parsimonious** life

paternalist (adj.)
= **relating to the practice by rulers of limiting the freedom of those being ruled (purportedly for the good of the latter)** from the Latin *pater*: father

e.g. After Saddam Hussein's removal, the US waited for such a long time before allowing democratic elections in Iraq that accusations of **paternalist** behaviour abounded

pathetic fallacy (phrase)
= **the attribution in artistic works of human feelings to non-human things** *for etymology, see box opposite*

e.g. Novelists are fond of using **pathetic fallacy**; an example can be found in the use of the expression 'the sky is weeping' instead of the more conventional 'it is raining'

---

pathetic fallacy is composed of the Greek word pathos, meaning 'the quality that arouses pity', and the Latin word fallere: to deceive.

As a *pathetic fallacy* refers to depicting non-human things in a human light (which is a popular activity of artists), it is no surprise that it was an art critic, John Ruskin, who coined the term, noting in his book **Modern Painters** (1856) that the pathetic fallacy had as its aim 'to signify any description of inanimate natural objects that ascribes to them human capabilities...'

An everyday example of a *pathetic fallacy* is when someone looks up and says of the rain falling from above: 'the sky is weeping'.

pathological (adj.)
= **caused by a disease** from the Greek *pathos*: suffering, disease, and *logos*: word

e.g. Sportsmen who reach world number one are usually **pathologically** competitive

patina (noun)
= **a surface that has changed due to age** from the Latin *patina*: a shallow dish (*which is an example of a piece of crockery prone to incrustations caused by the passing of time*)

e.g. The face of a 90 year old is etched with a **patina** of fine lines and wrinkles

patrician (adj.)

= **belonging to an illustrious and wealthy family** from the Latin *patricius*: having a noble father

e.g. Danielle Steel has no need for the riches from her 580m book sales for she was born into a **patrician** family

Pavlovian (adj.)

= **relating to a response that, over time, can be elicited by one stimulus alone (when at first two stimuli were needed)** *for etymology, see box below*

e.g. When I see my wife putting on her apron, I start salivating – before she has even touched any food – due to a **Pavlovian** response to that apron of hers

---

Pavlovian is an expression deriving from the work of Ivan Pavlov (1849–1936), a Russian scientist who won the Nobel Prize.

Pavlov noted that dogs salivate when food is presented to them; far more significantly, he also noticed that – if you ring a bell seconds before presenting the food – eventually the bell alone will be enough to produce the salivation (even if no food is ever presented).

*Thus Pavlov concluded that some responses by an animal are based on that animal's previous experiences (and are not just based on an animal's reflexes). Today, we use the word **Pavlovian** to describe any response within us that we can only explain owing to a past experience coming to the fore (rather than owing to our reaction to a present stimulus outside of ourselves).*

pellucid (adj.)
= *(of a concept)* **easily grasped** from the Latin *perlucere*: to shine through, from *per-*: through, and *lucere*: to shine

e.g. Ernest Hemingway wrote such simple sentences that his novels are considered amongst the most **pellucid** in the English language

penitential (adj.)
= **repentant** from the Latin *paenitentia*: repentance

e.g. Victims of fraudster Bernard Madoff were angry that he didn't appear more **penitential** in court

penurious (adj.)
= **very poor** from the Latin *penuria*: need

e.g. There are many charities set up in order to help **penurious** families

perdition (noun)
= **hell** *(in Christian teaching)* from the Latin *perditio*: ruin; *perdition* literally means 'utter ruin'

e.g. Many people who start off by abusing soft drugs like marijuana end up in the **perdition** of heroin addiction

peremptory (adj.)
= *(of a person's manner)* **insisting on total subservience** from the Latin *peremptorius*: decisive, from *perimere*: to take away (from *per-*: completely, and *emere*: to procure)

e.g. Elvis Presley once insisted on flying 500 miles in his jet to collect a peanut butter sandwich; his staff complied, afraid to refuse his **peremptory** request

perfunctory (adj.)
= *(of an action)* **done carelessly, as a matter of routine**
from the Latin *perfunctorius*: careless

e.g. *Breakfast at Tiffany*'s author Truman Capote hated
writing so postponed it by sharpening pencils for hours:
he found this **perfunctory** action soothing

peripatetic (adj.)
= **travelling around from place to place** from the Greek *peripatetikos*: walking about, from the verb *peripatein*: to walk about

e.g. Richard Branson is a **peripatetic** man who seems as likely to be in a hot air balloon halfway across the Atlantic as he is to be in London

peroration (noun)
= **the final part of a speech (that is intended to inspire enthusiasm in the audience)** from the Latin *perorare*: to speak at length, from *per-*: through, and *orare*: to speak

e.g. David Cameron's speeches often culminate in a stirring **peroration**

perspicacious (adj.)
= **having a clear insight into things** from the Latin *perspicare*: to see clearly, from *per-*: through, and *specere*: to look

e.g. Leonardo da Vinci was a **perspicacious** individual who was not just a painter but also the designer of several flying machines

phalanx (noun)

= a group of similar-looking people or things
for etymology, see box below

e.g. When Arthur Conan Doyle killed off Sherlock Holmes in his short story *The Final Problem*, a **phalanx** of grief-stricken fans wearing black armbands protested outside his home

---

phalanx is an ancient Greek word used to describe a group of soldiers who formed a defensive unit by packing themselves tightly together, overlapping their shields and extending their spears.

Today, we continue to use this word to describe any group of people who look the same and stay close together – such as photographers awaiting a celebrity at a film premiere, or bodyguards surrounding a president.

*The plural of this word is **phalanxes**. Note though that there is an alternative plural, which is **phalanges** – and this has a different meaning, which is 'bones of the finger or toe':*

*e.g. If a footballer fractures his **phalanges**, he is out of action for weeks*

---

phantasmagorical (adj.)

= relating to a sequence of surreal images as if from a dream from the French *fantasme*: phantasm

e.g. Lothario Errol Flynn observed that women would watch his films, create a **phantasmagorical** image of him, and then try a 'direct confrontation' with him

pharisaic (adj.)
= **self-righteous and punctilious** *for etymology, see box below*

e.g. Politicians who denounce adultery while themselves having affairs are **pharisaic**

> The word **pharisaic** *derives from the Pharisees, an ancient Jewish sect notorious for their strictness and sense of superiority.*
>
> *In the New Testament, the Pharisees are presented as rule-followers, in contrast to Jesus who is concerned only with expressing God's love. For example, the Pharisees ostracise sinners, whereas Jesus actively seeks them out.*
>
> *Today, we use the word* **pharisaic** *to refer to anyone who displays self-righteousness in their obsession with following the rules.*

phlegmatic (adj.)
= *(of a person)* **having a disposition that cannot be perturbed** *for etymology, see box below*

e.g. The Dalai Lama has a permanent smile which gives him a **phlegmatic** air

---

*Nowadays, **phlegm** is used to mean 'mucus discharged from the mouth'. However, the ancient Greeks used the word differently: for them, **phlegm** was one of four body fluids that account for our mood (the Greek word was* phlegma, *meaning 'an inflammation', reflecting the fact that phlegm was also supposed to be the cause of many diseases).*

***Phlegm** was believed to be associated with a calm, near apathetic – temperament. This sense persists in the meaning of the word **phlegmatic** today, which we use to describe someone who does not get rattled easily.*

---

physiognomy (noun)
= **a person's facial features, especially when regarded as reflecting that person's character** from the Greek *phusiognomonia*: judging of a man's nature (by his features), based on *physio-*: nature, and *gnomon*: a judge

e.g. Research shows aggressive people tend to have particularly wide faces (due to high testosterone levels): this is proof of the value of **physiognonomy**

picaresque (adj.)
= **relating to an episodic style of fiction dealing with the adventures of a dishonest but likeable hero** from the Spanish, *picaro*: rogue

e.g. *The Adventures of Huckleberry Finn* by Mark Twain can be described as a picaresque novel because it covers the life of a roguish hero of lowly social status who lives by his wits; *The White Tiger* by Aravind Adiga is a modern-day example

plangent (adj.)
= *(of a sound)* **like a lament** from the Latin *plangere*: to lament

e.g. One billion people worldwide watched Michael Jackson's funeral, at which Stevie Wonder sung in **plangent** tones

pluralistic (adj.)
= **relating to a system in which two or more groups live side by side** from the Latin *plus*, *plur-*: more

e.g. Muslims live alongside Christians in Britain – proof that we live in a **pluralistic** society

plutocrat (noun)
= **a person whose power is due to their wealth** from the Greek *ploutos*: wealth, and *kratos*: rule

e.g. The Prime Minister of Italy, Silvio Berlusconi, is also a billionaire who controls several TV channels: hence his being labelled a **plutocrat** by journalists

poleaxed (verb)
= **to have received a huge shock** deriving from the word *poleaxe*: a short-handled axe with a spike at the back; *poleaxed literally means 'as if struck by a poleaxe'*

e.g. As a child, horror writer Stephen King witnessed a friend being run over by a train: the experience left him **poleaxed**

polemic

polemic (noun)
= **a strong verbal assault on someone or something** from the Greek *polemos*: war

e.g. After he was convicted of the rape of Desiree Washington, Miss Black Rhode Island, the press launched a **polemic** against Mike Tyson

Pollyanna (noun)
= **a person who is overly optimistic** *for etymology, see box below*

e.g. Judy Garland got divorced from no less than four husbands but still decided to marry a fifth time: this undented optimism proves she was a **Pollyanna**

Pollyanna originates from the name of the main character in Eleanor H. Porter's bestselling novel, Pollyanna, *which was published in 1913.*

In the novel, Pollyanna, an orphan, goes to live with her austere aunt in a New England town in America. Pollyanna is an optimistic type who enjoys playing a game her father taught her, which involves trying to spot a good side to everything. Eventually her optimism proves infectious, transforming the town into a happy place.

Today, we continue to describe anyone with such a relentlessly optimistic attitude as being a **Pollyanna**.

---

polyglot (adj.)
= **knowing many languages** from the Greek *polu-*: many, and *glotta*: tongue

e.g. Rowan Williams, the Archbishop of Canterbury, talks with ease to the leaders of other world faiths because he is **polyglot**

polymath (noun)
= **a person who has much knowledge** from the Greek *polumathes*: having learned much, from *polu-*: much (the stem of *manthanein*: to learn)

e.g. Leonardo da Vinci was not only a consummate painter, but he was also an inventor who designed military machines such as rapid-firing cannons: he was a true **polymath**

polyphonic (adj.)
= **producing many sounds at the same time** from the Greek *poluphonos*, from *polu-*: many, and *phone*: voice

e.g. At the age of two, Mozart paid a visit to a farm and, from amidst the **polyphonic** backdrop, identified a pig's grunt as being in G-sharp

popinjay (noun)
= **a vain person** from the Old French *papegai*: a parrot

e.g. With his foppish outfits and tousled hair, Oscar Wilde was a clear example of a **popinjay**

porcine (adj.)
= **like a pig** from the Latin *porcinus*: a pig

e.g. Dr Robert Atkins invented a low carbohydrate diet to rid himself of his own **porcine** appearance

portentous (adj.)
= **relating to a warning that something bad is set to occur** from the Latin *portentum*: an omen; *portentous literally means 'constituting a portent or omen'*

e.g. The chief executive addressed his staff in a portentous tone, not realising that most of them were uninterested in his message and in fact daydreaming

portico (noun)
= **a porch consisting of a roof supported by columns spaced out at regular intervals** from the Latin *porticus*: porch

e.g. The Royal Opera House in London has a façade consisting of a giant **portico**

portmanteau word (phrase)
= **a word that has been created by blending the sounds and meanings from two or more words** from the French *porter*: to carry, and *manteau*: coat; *portmanteau literally means 'a large suitcase that opens into two hinged halves'*

e.g. *Brunch* is a **portmanteau word** coined from combining the words *breakfast* and *lunch*

potentate (noun)
= **a ruler, especially one who takes no account of other people's desires** from the Latin *potens*: powerful

e.g. The cringe-inducing character played by Ricky Gervais in the TV series *The Office* is a **potentate** who is blind to his own flaws

prehensile (adj.)
= *(of a human or animal)* **capable of grasping** from the Latin *prehendere*: to grasp

e.g. Many bank directors responsible for the credit crunch continue to hang on to their seats with what George Orwell called '**prehensile** bottoms'

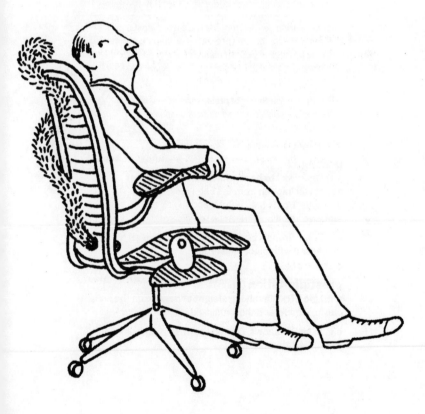

prelapsarian (adj.)
= **in a pure and unspoiled state** *for etymology, see box below*

e.g. Bankers often fondly remember their bonuses during **prelapsarian** years leading up to the Lehman Brothers' collapse

> *prelapsarian derives from the Latin word* lapsus *and literally means 'before (pre-) the Fall (lapsus)', referring to the passage in Genesis about the fall of humankind into a state of sin owing to Adam and Eve disobeying God by eating the apple in the Garden of Eden.*
>
> *Today, we use the word **prelapsarian** to evoke that period of our lives when a state of unspoiled innocence prevailed.*

presage (verb)
= *(of an event)* **to be an indication that another event will happen** from the Latin *praesagire*: to forebode, from *prae-*: before, and *sagire*: to perceive keenly

e.g. Frank Bruno's bizarre behaviour **presaged** his being diagnosed with bipolar disorder

prestidigitation (noun)
= **magic tricks involving sleight of hand** from the French *preste*: nimble, and the Latin *digitus*: finger

e.g. In his TV shows, Derren Brown demonstrates acts of **prestidigitation**

preternatural (adj.)
= **beyond what is natural** from the Latin *praeter*: beyond, and *natura*: nature

e.g. Simon Cowell, inventor of *The X Factor*, has a **preternatural** ability to provide the public with what it wants

priapic (adj.)
= **relating to male sexual activity** *for etymology, see box below*

e.g. On their marriage night, *War and Peace* author Leo Tolstoy forced his wife to read extracts from his diaries detailing his prior **priapic** experiences

---

priapic derives from the name of Priapos, who was the Greek god of male genitalia and fertility. The Greek myth surrounding Priapos is a particularly salacious one and goes as follows:

His mother, Aphrodite, when pregnant with Priapos, won a beauty competition. The goddess who lost out to Aphrodite was so annoyed that she proceeded to curse Aphrodite's son, Priapos – who was still in the womb – to be born with a foul mind. As a result, when Priapos emerged into the world, he had an erection that would never subside.

Today, we continue to refer to oversexed males as being **priapic***.*

---

primordial (adj.)
= *(of a quality)* **so fundamental as to have existed from the start of time** from the Latin *primordialis*: first of all, from *primus*: first, and *ordiri*: to begin

e.g. Any good ruler understands that his subjects require food and lodging, for these are mankind's **primordial** needs

Procrustean (adj.)

= **enforcing uniformity and stamping out individual quirks** from the Greek *prokroustes*: stretcher; *for etymology, see box below*

e.g. Some people do believe in God but do not belong to a particular religion because they find the associated rules and regulations **Procrustean**

Procrustean derives from the name of Procrustes, a torturer in Greek mythology.

Procrustes would force his victims back to his house to try out his bed for size. If they were too long for the bed, he would chop their legs off; if they were too short, he would stretch their limbs. In the event that someone was the perfect fit for his bed, Procrustes had a differently-proportioned bed that he kept in reserve and would produce the one that was the worse fit for his victim, thus guaranteeing some form of torture would ensue.

*Today, we call someone **Procrustean** if they try to fit people into excessively narrow limits with no regard for individuality.*

---

profligate (adj.)

= **ruinously extravagant** from the Latin *profligare*: to ruin

e.g. F. Scott Fitzgerald, author of *The Great Gatsby*, was so **profligate** that he would light his cigarettes with flaming five-dollar bills

proliferate (verb)

= **to increase quickly in number** from the Latin *proles*: offspring, and *ferre*: to carry

e.g. Pete Sampras won the US Open at the age of 19; from this point onwards, his list of Grand Slam wins **proliferated** rapidly

prolix (adj.)
= *(of speech or writing)* **using too many words** from the Latin *prolixus*: poured forth, from *pro-*: outward, and *liquere*: to be liquid

e.g. Legal contracts are often **prolix** and so send most people to sleep

promulgate (verb)
= *(of an ideal)* **to make known far and wide** from the Latin *promulgare*, from *pro-*: out, and *mulgare*: to cause to come forth; *'promulgate' literally means 'to milk'*

e.g. The disciples found Jesus's sermons so compelling that they set out to **promulgate** his teachings

propagate (verb)
= **to cause to spread** from the Latin *propagare*: to multiply from layers or shoots, from *propago*: a young shoot; *propagate literally means 'to reproduce by natural processes from the parent stock'*

e.g. Actor Richard Gere **propagates** AIDS awareness around the world

propitious (adj.)
= **indicating a fair chance of success** from the Latin *propitius*: favourable

e.g. Björn Borg would sport a beard when playing at Wimbledon because he believed that not shaving was **propitious**

proselytise (verb)

= **to convert (someone) from one belief to another** from the Greek *proselutos*: a stranger or convert

e.g. Christian missionary work has as its main goal that of **proselytising** non-believers

protean (adj.)

= **able to transform easily** *for etymology, see box below*

e.g. The pop singer Madonna is a **protean** performer who undergoes frequent image transformations

---

protean originates from the name of Proteus, a sea god in Greek mythology who could prophesy the future.

People came from far and wide to ask Proteus about their fates. However, they were frequently disappointed, for Proteus's quirk was that he disliked being asked direct questions so much that he would change shape in order to confuse these inquisitors.

*Today, we still describe someone as **protean** if they have the ability to change rapidly.*

---

prurient (adj.)

= **having an unhealthy interest in sexual matters: or encouraging sexual matters** from the Latin *prurire*: to itch, long

e.g. Errol Flynn had an active love life and he called his autobiography *My Wicked, Wicked Ways*, knowing this title would appeal to his **prurient** fan base

puckish (adj.)
= **playful in a mischievous manner** deriving from the Middle English *puke*: an evil spirit

e.g. Ian Fleming, the creator of *James Bond*, also wrote *Chitty Chitty Bang Bang* and other books for children to indulge his **puckish** side

pullulate (verb)
= **to breed quickly; OR to be pulsing with life** from the Latin *pullulare*: to sprout, from the diminutive of *pullus*: young animal; *pullulate literally means 'to breed so quickly as to become common'*

e.g. Immediately before a big match, ticket touts **pullulate** around football stadiums

punctilious (adj.)
= **showing huge attention to detail** from the French *pointaille*: detail

e.g. Kingsley Amis would often write 500 words in **punctilious** fashion before drinking at lunchtime

(purdah) go into purdah

(purdah) go into purdah (phrase)
= **to go into social seclusion** *for etymology, see box below*

e.g. After allegations of his infidelity surfaced, Tiger Woods went into self-imposed **purdah**

---

purdah originates from the Persian word parda, *which means 'a curtain', reflecting the Hindu or Muslim practice of 'purdah' which involved hiding women from the view of men.*

'Purdah' is achieved either by the separation of the sexes or by women covering themselves with a 'burqa', which is a long, loose garment that covers the body from head to toe.

*Today, we use the phrase **go into purdah** to describe any instance of social seclusion, an activity most often practised by privacy-seeking celebrities.*

---

purgative (adj.)
= **ridding someone of unpleasant feelings** from the Latin *purgare*: to purify; *purgative literally means 'having the effect of a strong laxative'*

e.g. People who have received a shock often find alcohol **purgative**

purple prose (phrase)
= **prose that is excessively ornate** *for etymology, see box opposite*

e.g. Barbara Cartland might have shifted 500m copies of her romantic novels, but critics didn't like her writing, describing it as **purple prose**

purple prose was a term used by the Romans to describe fancy writing.

The phrase came about because, in Roman times, purple dye was very expensive to manufacture because it necessitated the crushing of tens of thousands of molluscs (types of shellfish). Consequently, it was only the Emperor and the very wealthy who could afford purple garments. However, certain social climbers developed the habit of sewing small bits of purple onto their robes to give themselves a 'touch of class'. This activity was considered pretentious.

*In 65 BC, the poet Horace harnessed the negative connotations of the colour purple when he described pretentious writing as **purple** and this phrase is still used today.*

purview (noun)
= **the extent of the influence (of someone or of something)** from the Old French *purveu*: foreseen

e.g. Many decisions carried out by the government are determined by ministers and do not come within the **purview** of the Prime Minister at all

pusillanimous (adj.)
= **timid** from the Latin *pusillanimis*, from *pusillus*: very small, and *animus*: mind

e.g. The character of *James Bond* is that of the alpha male: when you are hunting down terrorists, no **pusillanimous** streak can be indulged

putrefy (verb)
= **to rot, emitting an unpleasant smell** from the Latin *puter*: rotten

e.g. If you discard prawns in a dustbin, there is soon an overpowering smell of **putrefying** crustacea

quango (noun)

= **an agency that receives finance from a government while acting independently of it** *quango is based originally on the 1970s' US acronym of 'qua(si) n(on-) g(overnmental) o(rganisation)'*

e.g. The Press Complaints Commission (PCC) – to which the government has given the power to regulate all British newspapers – is a classic **quango**

quarry (noun)

= **an object of pursuit** from the Old French curée: quarry, a hunting term that referred to the refuse parts of a slain animal that were given to the hounds in its skin (*curée* being based on the French cuir, meaning 'skin')

e.g. After meeting Victoria Adams at a charity football match, David Beckham made her his **quarry** and eventually married her

quiddity (noun)

= **the 'whatness' or intrinsic nature of someone or something** from the medieval Latin *quidditas*: whatness, from *quid*: what

e.g. Certain novelists are so skilful that the reader feels he understands the singular **quiddity** of the lead character of the book better than that of his real-life spouse

quiescent (adj.)

= **lying still** from the Latin *quiescere*: to be still

e.g. Maltreated workers may stay **quiescent** for years but will eventually mount a strike

quixotic (adj.)
= **very idealistic and unrealistic** *for etymology, see box opposite*

e.g. It takes a **quixotic** individual – like actor Clark Gable – to believe in the institution of marriage sufficiently to attempt it six times

quixotic derives from the name of Don Quixote, the hero of the famous 17th-century Spanish novel of the same name by the author Miguel de Cervantes.

Don Quixote is a retired country gentleman who develops an obsession with tales of chivalry. Eventually he becomes delusional and, designating a neighbour as his squire and a farm girl as his ladylove, he embarks on a series of adventures. At the height of his madness he attacks some windmills, believing them to be giants. (Incidentally this episode is the genesis of our modern-day expression 'tilting at windmills', which means 'fighting an imaginary opponent').

Eventually he undergoes a return to sanity but is left feeling melancholic and dies a broken man. When we call someone **quixotic**, we mean they are like Don Quixote: full of grand chivalrous schemes but not living in the real world.

R

rabid (adj.)
= **raving** *for etymology, see box below*

e.g. Militant atheists depict fundamental Christians as being **rabid**

---

rabid derives from the Latin **rabere**, *which means 'to rave', and literally describes an animal made raving mad by rabies.*

We use the word figuratively to refer to a human who is 'foaming at the mouth' as they insist that their beliefs are correct; hence **rabid** *is often used to describe religious extremists.*

---

raillery (noun)
= **teasing of a light-hearted nature** from the French *raillery*: to rail

e.g. People who are in a grumpy mood can respond badly to **raillery**

rapacious (adj.)
= **snatching** from the Latin *rapacis*: snatching

e.g. Every year Arnold Schwarzenegger donates to charity his $175,000 salary as governor of California: he seems the opposite of a **rapacious** Hollywood star

realpolitik (noun)

= **a system of politics based on a practical – rather than a moral – approach** from the German *Realpolitik*: practical politics; *for etymology, see box below*

e.g. Before he became Prime Minister, the press often accused David Cameron of tailoring his views to suit public opinion and of other instances of **realpolitik**

---

realpolitik refers to the implementation of a form of politics that is pragmatic – often at the expense of moral considerations.

*The first practitioner of **realpolitik** was Otto von Bismarck, Chancellor to Wilhelm I of the Kingdom of Prussia (a landmass covering parts of Germany and Russia); for example, keen to ensure the election of a Pope favourable to his own political aims, von Bismarck had no qualms about attempting to manipulate the Papal elections during the 1870s.*

Modern proponents include Richard Nixon who, for example, tolerated the human rights' violations of China as this meant greater global stability.

*Today, when we describe someone as practising **realpolitik**, we mean they are pragmatic – rather than principled – individuals: in other words, they are **Machiavellian*** (see p. 119).

---

rebarbative (adj.)

= **unpleasant-looking and aggressive** from the Old French *se rebarber*: to face each other 'beard to beard' in an aggressive fashion

e.g. When Marlon Brando became depressed in old age, his weight ballooned and his appearance became **rebarbative**

recalcitrant (adj.)
= **refusing to cooperate with authority** from the Latin *recalcitrare*: to kick out with the heels, based on *calx*: a heel

e.g. Most men end up married despite initially feeling **recalcitrant** towards the institution

recidivistic (adj.)
= *(of a convicted criminal)* **tending to relapse into crime** from the Latin *recidivus*: falling back, from the verb *recidere*, from *re-*: back, and *cadere*: to fall

e.g. Although the outlaw Jesse James carried out numerous successful heists, he was never satisfied with his takings, which led to his **recidivistic** behaviour

recondite (adj.)
= **not well known** from the Latin *reconditus*: hidden

e.g. *Schott's Original Miscellany* is full of information of a **recondite** nature

recusant (adj.)
= **defying an authority** from the Latin *recusans*: refusing

e.g. Many teenagers object to eating meals at the dining table and are generally **recusant**

redound to (verb)
= **to contribute (to a person's reputation)** from the Latin *redundare*: to overflow, from *re-*: again, and *unda*: a wave

e.g. Salvador Dali would shave his armpits until they bled in the hope he'd appeal more to females; this act of masochism **redounds to** his reputation as a man who adored women

refulgent (adj.)
= **shining** from the Latin *refulgere*: to shine out, from *re-* (an intensifying prefix) and *fulgere*: to shine

e.g. As Lord Sugar's chauffeur pulled up outside the building, the car's metalwork was **refulgent** in the sunlight

reliquary (noun)
= **a container for relics** from the Old French *relique*: relic

e.g. Before admitting they would never fit her again, the fat woman tried on some outfits from her **reliquary** of 'thin' clothes

rescind (verb)
= **to revoke (an arrangement)** from the Latin *re-* (an intensifying prefix), and *scindere*: to divide

e.g. Obama has **rescinded** some laws created by Bush

residuum (noun)
= **a thing that is left behind after a process** from the Latin *residuus*: remaining

e.g. Grace Kelly is dead but her **residuum** of films continues to exist

retroussé (adj.)
= *(of the nose)* **turned up** from the French *re-*: back, and *trousser*: to turn

e.g. Rumours abounded that Michael Jackson had plastic surgery because the passing of the years saw his nose become increasingly **retroussé**

rhapsodise about (phrase)
= **to talk about a topic with great passion** from the Greek *rhapsodos*: a bard who recites poetry *(literally meaning 'someone who stitches songs together')*, from *rhaptein*: to stitch, and *oide*: song

e.g. It is obvious from interviews that Prince Charles is in love with his wife Camilla because he often **rhapsodises about** her

ribald (adj.)
= **referring to sex in a funny but rude way** from the Old French *riber*: to indulge in licentious pleasures

e.g. Frank Sinatra was popular with the ladies and, after a few drinks, would boast about his sexual exploits in a **ribald** way

rictus (noun)
= **a gaping grin** from the Latin *rictus*: a gaping of the jaws of an animal, from the past participle of the verb *ringi*: to gape

e.g. In photos Bill Clinton always seems to have a cheery demeanour, which is largely due to a permanent **rictus**

riparian (adj.)
= **situated on a riverbank** from the Latin *ripa*: bank

e.g. Many paintings from the impressionist era feature couples picnicking against a **riparian** backdrop

rococo (adj.)
= **ornate in a tasteless way** *for etymology, see box below*

e.g. The press likes to depict the large houses of Premier League footballers as tasteless blends of **rococo** features

---

rococo describes many different forms of art, including music, architecture and woodwork.

The rococo movement reached its peak in 18th-century Continental Europe and was characterised in furniture design by ornate spiral lines – hence the word's etymology from the French la rocaille, *which means 'a garden made of rocks' (another example of an elaborate manmade creation).*

Examples of rococo art include the Palace of Versailles and the music of Vivaldi. Today, we continue to describe any intricate artwork as rococo.

---

roué (adj.)
= **a sex-obsessed old man** *for etymology, see box opposite*

e.g. After his trial for relations with a minor, Errol Flynn attached this notice to his door: 'Ladies: be prepared to produce your birth certificate'. What a **roué**!

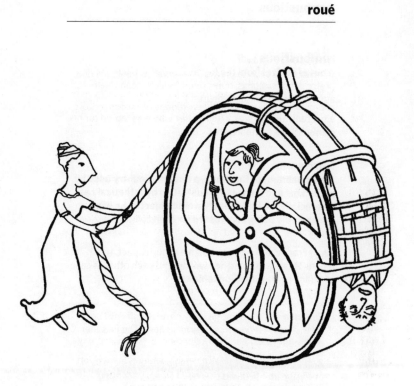

The word **roué** has an interesting story behind it: in 18th century France, men who consorted with much younger women were punished by having their backs broken over a wheel (**une roue**). Today, we continue to describe dirty old men as **roués**.

rumbustious (adj.)

= **out of control** from the Icelandic, *ram-* (an intensifying prefix), and *bunctious*: bumptious (which means 'self-assertive to an irritating degree')

e.g. Frank Sinatra was a hell-raiser who was famed for his **rumbustious** comportment

Ruritanian (noun)

= **an inhabitant of Ruritania, a fictional country used by politicians and lawyers to illustrate a hypothetical case – especially if a real country would object to be used in the example being considered** *for etymology, see box below*

e.g. If France and Germany sign a security pact, this means these two countries will defend each other in case of attack by, say, the **Ruritanians**

Ruritania was the name given by novelist Anthony Pope to a fictitious European country in his novel The Prisoner of Zenda *(1894).*

*Within literature, the word **Ruritania** has since been used to conjure up a fictitious country in Europe abounding with fairytale notions of chivalry and romance (as per Pope's novel). For example, Evelyn Waugh describes one character in his novel* Vile Bodies *as a sad 'ex-King of Ruritania'.*

*Today, the fictional country of **Ruritania** is most often used in a more practical context: namely by politicians and lawyers to illustrate a hypothetical case – especially if a real country would object to being used in the example being considered.*

salient (adj.)
= **prominent** from the Latin *salient-*: leaping (from the verb *salire*); *salient literally means 'pointing outward'*

e.g. Thomas Jefferson was responsible for the invention of the coat hanger but he is remembered for being the US President because this is the **salient** fact of his life

sangfroid (noun)
= **composure under pressure** from the French *sang-froid*: cold blood

e.g. Rugby star Jonny Wilkinson's **sangfroid** explains his ability to penalty kick under pressure

sanguinary (adj.)
= **involving the spilling of much blood** from the Latin *sanguis, sanguinis*: blood

e.g. *Vlad the Impaler* (1431–1476) would murder his victims in particularly **sanguinary** ways as he liked to drink their blood after killing them

sanguine (adj.)
= **optimistic** from the Latin *sanguis, sanguinis*: blood; *sanguine literally means 'bloody in colour'*

e.g. After divorcing his fifth wife, actor Clark Gable was **sanguine** about his chances of finding love again: sure enough, he soon found wife number six

sardonic (adj.)

= **dourly cynical** *for etymology, see box below*

e.g. Comedian Lewis Grizzard once **sardonically** commented: 'Instead of getting married again, I'm going to find a woman I don't like and just give her a house'

---

*sardonic derives from the ancient Greeks' belief that eating a certain plant from the country of **Sardo** (which was the Greeks' name for Sardinia) would cause facial contortions that resembled those of sardonic laughter; death usually followed.*

*Today, we continue to use **sardonic** to mean 'grimly cynical'; and 'gallows humour' (i.e. humour arising from life-threatening situations) is one manifestation of a sardonic sense of humour.*

saturnine (adj.)

= *(of a person)* **slow and dark (in colouring) and melancholic** *for etymology, see box below*

e.g. Henry VIII's weight gain in old age made him slow and depressed: he had become **saturnine**

Saturnine derives from the medieval Latin Saturninus, which means 'of Saturn'.

In medieval times, Saturn was considered by astrologers to be the coldest and darkest of the planets because it was thought to be the furthest from the sun.

*When we describe someone as **saturnine** today, we summon up these negative qualities.*

scabrous (adj.)
= **indecent** from the Latin *scaber*: rough; *scabrous literally means 'covered with scabs'*

e.g. The media are fond of quoting John F. Kennedy's **scabrous** comment: 'If I don't have a woman for three days, I get terrible headaches'

scatological (adj.)
= **concerning excrement** from the Greek *skor, skatos*: excrement, and *logos*: word

e.g. Although some adults find fart jokes amusing, most people outgrow their **scatological** sense of humour of their youth

schadenfreude (noun)
= **the pleasure experienced when someone other than you has a mishap** from the German *Schaden*: harm, and *freude*: joy

e.g. When Emperor Nero's wife pointed out he was late for dinner, he kicked her to death; on hearing this news, not even her fiercest enemies felt **schadenfreude**

scintilla (noun)
= **no more than a spark of a feeling** from the Latin *scintilla*: spark

e.g. He may have started as the underdog in the Tory leadership race in 2005, but David Cameron's faith in his speech-making ability gave him a **scintilla** of hope

sclerotic (adj.)
= **rigid, unable to adapt** from the Greek *skleros*: hard; *sclerotic literally means 'becoming rigid'*

e.g. The marriage between Marie Antoinette and Louis XVI wasn't consummated until its seventh year: theirs was a **sclerotic** relationship

scrofulous (adj.)
= **relating to a form of tuberculosis that produces glandular swellings; OR morally degenerate** from the Latin *scrofulae*: a swelling of the glands (diminutive of *scrofa*: a sow, which was said to be subject to the disease)

e.g. The squalid environment of some jails abroad can make the inmates **scrofulous**

sedition (noun)
= **conduct inciting people to overthrow an authority** from the Latin *seditio*, from *sed-*: apart, and *itio*: going (from the verb *ire*: to go)

e.g. Hitler used force to quell **sedition**

sedulous (adj.)
= **showing diligence** from the Latin *sedulus*: zealous

e.g. Mother Teresa worked **sedulously** to alleviate the suffering of the poor

segue (verb)
= **to make a smooth transition from one thing to another** from the Italian *segue*: follows

e.g. After retiring from acting, Paul Newman **segued** successfully into the business world, creating a profitable empire from making cooking sauces

seismic (adj.)
= **of earth-shattering proportions** from the Greek *seismos*: earthquake

e.g. The events of September the 11th, 2001 had a **seismic** impact on world peace for years afterwards

seminal (adj.)
= **strongly influencing future developments** from the Latin *seminalis*, from *semen*: seed; *seminal literally means 'relating to semen'*

e.g. After being rejected for a job at the Foreign Office, Ian Fleming decided to create his alter ego, James Bond: so this snub was the **seminal** moment in the spy's creation

semiotics (noun)
= **the study of signs and symbols** from the Greek *semeloun*: to interpret as a sign

e.g. In the novel *The Da Vinci Code*, a professor of **semiotics** at Harvard uses his knowledge to solve a series of puzzles and unearth a conspiracy

sententious (adj.)
= **given to expressing pompous opinions** from the Latin *sententia*: opinion

e.g. When they preach to their congregation, priests must avoiding sounding **sententious**

seraglio (noun)
= **the harem in a Muslim palace** from the Persian *saray*: palace

e.g. It would be no surprise to learn that Saddam Hussein's palace contained a **seraglio**

serendipitous (adj.)
= **relating to the occurrence of events by chance and with a positive outcome** *for etymology, see box below*

e.g. For his 12th birthday, Elvis Presley wanted a bike but his mother could only afford a guitar: this proved to be a **serendipitous** gift for someone as musically talented as 'The King'

---

serendipitous derives from the title of The Three Princes of Serendip, *the English version of a fairy tale published in Venice in 1557 and to which author Horace Walpole referred in a letter he wrote in 1754.*

In the story, the three princes had a habit of stumbling across good things, or, as Walpole put it: 'were always making discoveries, by accidents and sagacity, of things they were not in quest of'.

*Today, we use the word **serendipitous** to describe any chance event with a similarly joyful outcome.*

Shangri-La (noun)
= **an earthly paradise that is a retreat from the confusion of civilisation** *for etymology, see box opposite*

e.g. Oprah Winfrey lives on a huge Californian estate called 'The Promised Land', which overlooks the ocean: this is her own **Shangri-La**

Shangri-La is a fictional place described in the 1933 novel Lost Horizon *by James Hilton.*

In the novel, Shangri-La is a paradise in Tibet enclosed by mountains; its inhabitants have a peculiarly long lifespan and barely display signs of ageing.

Shangri-La is now used to denote any joyful land that is isolated from the outside world; it can also be used to denote a lifelong quest – for example, for a man who is obsessed with becoming prime minister, this goal is his Shangri-La.

shibboleth (noun)
= **a phrase or concept identified with a particular group**
for etymology, see box below

e.g. By using the **shibboleth** of a 'just war' to describe his invasion of Iraq, Tony Blair is attempting to frame his actions within a wider religious and historical context

shibboleth originates from a particularly bloody account in the Old Testament. In this passage (Judges 12:6), the Gileadites are pursuing the fleeing Ephraimites, whom the Gileadites have just defeated in battle. To identify a man as an Ephraimite, the Gileadites would ask him to say the word shibboleth (which means 'an ear of corn' in Hebrew); the Ephraimites could not pronounce this word correctly because they lacked a 'sh' sound in their dialect. Ephraimites would therefore fail the pronunciation test and then be slaughtered.

Today, shibboleth is used to describe any phrase particular to a narrow group of people (such as 'credit derivatives', a phrase only bankers would claim to understand) or an experience common to one group (such as circumcision in the Jewish faith).

sibilant (adj.)
= **sounding like a hiss** from the Latin *sibilare*: to hiss

e.g. The phrase 'she sells seashells by the seashore' is particularly **sibilant**

simian (adj.)
= **like a monkey** from the Latin *simia*: an ape

e.g. When Charles Darwin published his book *On the Origin of Species* in 1859, newspapers responded by printing cartoons of Darwin in a **simian** guise

simpatico (adj.)
= *(of a person)* **likeable** from the Italian *simpatico*: sympathetic

e.g. Michael Parkinson was an effective chat show host because he put guests at ease with his **simpatico** manner

simper (verb)
= **to smile in a flirty fashion** from the German *zimpfer*: delicate

e.g. Julia Roberts became an international sex symbol due to her role in the film *Pretty Woman* (1990) in which she **simpered** continually at the camera

simulacrum (noun)
= **a representation of someone or something (usually a poor representation)** from the Latin *simulacrum*: a representation

e.g. The 2008 film of *Brideshead Revisited* was panned by critics as an inferior **simulacrum** of the book

slough off (verb)
= **to peel off (an old skin)** deriving from the Low German *slu(we)*: peel

e.g. As a result of his army service in Afghanistan, Prince Harry succeeded in **sloughing off** his 'playboy' image

smorgasbord (noun)
= **a wide range of something** from the Swedish *smörgås*: slice of bread and butter, and *bord*: table; *a smorgasbord literally refers to a buffet offering a variety of foods*

e.g. Baptism and confession are regarded by atheists as parts of a **smorgasbord** of religious superstitions

sobriquet (noun)
= **a nickname** from the Old French *sobriquet*: a tap under the chin, from *sous*: under, and *briquet*: throat

e.g. Owing to his command of language, novelist Henry James received the **sobriquet** 'the Master'

sodality (noun)
= **a fraternity of people** from the Latin *sodalis*: comrade

e.g. The villains in Dan Brown's novel *The Da Vinci Code* are members of Opus Dei, a real-life Roman Catholic **sodality**

soigné (adj.)
= **maintaining a polished experience** from the French *soigné*: taken care of

e.g. In his heyday, actor Roger Moore was renowned for his **soigné** good looks

solecism (noun)
= *(in speech)* **a grammatical error** from the Greek *soloikos*: speaking incorrectly

e.g. Some people think it is a **solecism** to split the infinitive, such as in the phrase 'to really work hard'

solipsistic (adj.)
= **obsessed with one's own feelings** from the Latin *solus*:
alone, and *ipse*: self

e.g. Truman Capote so admired an article about himself
that he wallpapered his flat with 500 copies of the
magazine in question: how **solipsistic** of him

sop (noun)
= **something given to pacify (such as a bribe)** *for
etymology, see box below*

e.g. Bankers, at government-supported banks, complain
that plans to cut their bonuses are a **sop** to angry
taxpayers, say critics

---

*A **sop** meant 'bread dipped in liquid' in Middle English.
The current sense of **sop** as being something designed to
pacify someone came from the epic poem* **The Aeneid**
written by Virgil (70–19 BC).

At one point in **The Aeneid**, *the hero Aeneas decides to
enter the underworld to see his dead father. Aeneas
consults the guardian to the underworld, a prophetess
called 'the Sibyl'. Knowing that the underworld is patrolled
by a monstrous dog 'the Sibyl' prepares a **sop** soaked in
honey and drugs to stupefy this animal; the plan works
and the **sop** renders the dog comatose.*

*Hence, today, a **sop** continues to mean 'something given
to pacify' and often describes a small thing done as a
concession to appease someone whose main demands are
not being met.*

---

sophistry (noun)
= **the use of unsound arguments, especially with the intention of outwitting someone** from the Greek *sophistes*: a sophist (a person who reasons with witty but unsound arguments)

e.g. When clients asked fraudster Bernard Madoff about his investment strategies, Madoff would use complicated language and **sophistry** to confuse them

sororal (adj.)
= **of or like a sister** from the Latin *soror*: sister

e.g. Tennis stars Venus and Serena Williams enjoy a healthy **sororal** rivalry

specious (adj.)
= **seeming plausible, but actually incorrect** from the Latin *speciosus*: fair

e.g. When Daniel Craig appeared as the new James Bond in *Casino Royale*, reports that Pierce Brosnan would continue in the role were proved **specious**

splenetic (adj.)
= **bad-tempered** *for etymology, see box opposite*

e.g. Inspector Morse's perpetual whisky-induced hangover perhaps explained why he was so **splenetic**

splenetic *derives from the Latin word splen, which means 'spleen'. This is because the ancient Greeks believed that the spleen – which is an organ involved in the creation and removal of blood cells – produced black bile which could darken someone's mood.*

Today, we continue to describe someone as **splenetic** *if that person is in a strop.*

spoonerism (noun)
= an error in speech when the initial sounds of two or more words are transposed, often to comic effect *for etymology, see below*

e.g. The teacher meant to say 'you have missed the history lectures' but it came out as 'you have hissed the mystery lectures'; the class erupted in laughter at his **spoonerism**

spoonerism *is a term that takes its name from an English clergyman and scholar called William Archibald Spooner (1844 and 1930).*

Reverend Spooner was notorious for confusing the letters at the start of adjacent words. For example, he is alleged to have said in church: 'The Lord is my shoving leopard'.

Today, we use the word **spoonerism** *to describe any instance of someone confusing the letters at the start of adjacent words.*

stentorian (adj.)

= *(of a person's voice)* **loud and strong** *for etymology, see box below*

e.g. Arnold Schwarzenegger was chosen to star in action films because of his muscular physique and **stentorian** voice

---

stentorian derives from the name of a man called Stentor, who in Greek mythology was the herald for the Greek forces during the Trojan War.

In his work **The Odyssey,** *Greek poet Homer notes that the loudness of Stentor's voice was equal to that of fifty men combined; however, Stentor's voice was not louder than a god's and he shouted himself to death during an unsuccessful attempt to defeat the god Hermes in a shouting contest.*

Today, the adjective **stentorian** *is used to describe someone with a booming voice.*

---

stucco (noun)

= **fine plaster used for coating walls or moulding into decorative features** from the Old German *stukki*: a fragment

e.g. *Hello* magazine often features photos of footballers' houses that have been made ornate by the use of **stucco**

Sturm und Drang (phrase)

= **unpleasant emotional turbulence** *for etymology, see box opposite*

e.g. During their teenage years most people are prone to **Sturm und Drang**

Sturm und Drang is a German expression meaning 'Storm and Stress'.

The ***Sturm und Drang*** movement originated in Germany at the end of the 18th century and involved the venting of spleen and anguish; this was as a reaction against the rigidity of the rationalism imposed by the Enlightenment movement. The most famous piece of literature of the time was Goethe's Die Leiden des jungen Werthers (The Suffering of Young Werther), a novel which describes a man so lovelorn that he kills himself.

Today, when we describe someone as suffering from ***Sturm und Drang***, we mean they are in a state of unpleasant emotional turmoil.

suborn (verb)
= **to bribe or otherwise persuade (someone) to commit a crime** from the Latin *subornare*: to incite secretly, from *sub-*: secretly, and *ornare*: to equip

e.g. To achieve their ends, politicians in Africa are often accused of **suborning** public institutions such as the media

sulphurous (adj.)
= **erupting with anger** *for etymology, see below*

e.g. In his heyday, John McEnroe's **sulphurous** comments to referees made for great newspaper stories

sulphurous literally means 'containing sulphur'; sulphur is a chemical with which gunpowder and other explosives are formed.

So, when we describe someone as ***sulphurous***, it means that person is about to explode with anger.

superannuated (adj.)

= **too old to be of use** from the Latin *super*: over, and *annus*: year

e.g. Though she is now in her 80s, the Queen continues to perform many duties with great efficiency: no one would say she is **superannuated**

supercilious (adj.)

= **behaving as though one thinks one is above other people** from the Latin *superciliosus*: haughty, from *supercilium*: eyebrow

e.g. **Supercilious** people have a manner that causes offence to others

supplicant (noun) / suppliant (adj.)

= *(of a person)* **making a humble plea to a leader** from the Latin *supplicare*: to implore

e.g. Spike Milligan once called Prince Charles a 'little grovelling bastard' on live TV as a joke: but it is clear from this that the comedian was no **supplicant**

suppurate (verb)

= **to form pus** from the Latin *sub-*: below, and *pus*, *puris*: pus

e.g. Some women who have breast augmentation operations experience **suppurating** wounds for days afterwards

susurrate (verb)

= **to murmur softly** from the Latin *susurrare*: to murmur

e.g. To judge by his manly appearance, you would expect footballer David Beckham to have a loud voice; yet in interviews he usually **susurrates**

Svengali (noun)
= **a person who controls another** *for etymology, see box below*

e.g. Simon Fuller has managed the Spice Girls and other celebrities, which resulted in the press giving him the title of 'management **Svengali'**

Svengali originates from the name of a character in the 1894 novel Trilby *by George du Maurier.*

In the book, Svengali is a character who uses hypnosis to control the singing voice of a weaker character called Trilby.

*Today, when we call someone a **Svengali**, we mean they are similarly controlling of someone else – usually in a sinister way.*

sybarite (noun)
= **a person who is overly fond of luxury** for etymology, see
box below

e.g. Charlie Chaplin used to frequent a brothel called *The
House of All Nations*, which was a popular haunt of
wealthy **sybarites**

---

*sybarite literally means 'an inhabitant of Sybarus'; Sybarus
was a city in Italy that existed in the 6th century BC.*

*Owing to the fertility of the surrounding soil, the
inhabitants of Sybarus were among the wealthiest people
in the world and were renowned for pampering
themselves: the city was sufficiently well off to install the
first streetlighting system in history.*

*Today, a **sybarite** is someone who has a fondness for
sensory indulgence.*

---

sylph (noun)
= **a thin female** from the Modern Latin *sylphes*: a spirit
inhabiting the air; *a sylph literally means 'an imaginary spirit
of the air'*

e.g. Despite being over 50 years old, Madonna retains the
appearance of a **sylph** as a result of her exercise regime

symposium (noun)
= **a meeting to discuss one topic in particular** from the
Latin *symposium* from the Greek *symposion*: an occasion
for drinking together, from *sun-*: together, and *potes*:
drinker

e.g. Samuel Beckett, author of *Waiting for Godot*, could go
for hours without saying a word: he was not someone to
seek out at a **symposium**

synaesthesia (noun)
= **the evocation of one sense by the stimulation of another sense** from the Greek *sun*: together, and *aesthesis*: sensation

e.g. Whenever I smell smoke from my uncle's pipe, I immediately think of my dead aunt playing the piano; this **synaesthesia** leaves me giddy

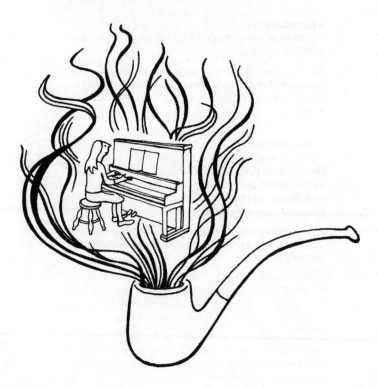

synapse (noun)
= **a connection between two nerve cells; to displace the beats in music so that strong beats become weak and weak beats become loud** from the Greek *sun*: together, and *hapsis*: joining

e.g. When a thought comes into our head, electricity travels across the **synapses** in our brain

syncopate (verb)
= **to shorten a word by dropping sounds in the word's middle** from the Latin *syncopare*: to swoon

e.g. People who think they are amusing when they **syncopate** words (such as by pronouncing the south London suburb of '*Clapham*' as '*Cla'hm*') are in fact annoying

synecdoche (noun)
= **a figure of speech in which a part is used to allude to the whole, or the whole is used to allude to a part** from the Greek *synekdokhe*: a receiving together, from *syn-*: with, *ek*: out, and *dekhesthai*: to receive (related to *dokein*: to seem good)

e.g. A thief notorious for his ability to pick pockets is often called 'Fingers', this term being a **synecdoche** for his body as a whole

tabula rasa (phrase)
= **the mind before it has been imprinted with the effects of experience** from the Latin *tabula*: tablet, and *rasa*: erased

e.g. The brain of a baby is a **tabula rasa** on to which the baby's parents etch their values

tangential (adj.)
= **digressing from a prior course** from the Latin *tangere*: to touch; *tangential literally means 'touching at a point without intersecting'*

e.g. Cameron and Osborne arranged a dinner to discuss the economy but ended up discussing **tangential** matters

Tartuffe (noun)
= **a hypocritical pretender to any kind of superiority** *for etymology, see box below*

e.g. J. Edgar Hoover, the first director of the FBI, called *Playboy* readers 'moral degenerates'; but he was a **Tartuffe** because he regularly watched pornographic films

---

Tartuffe is the lead character in the play Tartuffe, *written by the French playwright Molière in 1664.*

In the play, Tartuffe *persuades the other characters that he is pious and devout, whilst he is actually lustful and grasping. This rank hypocrisy is eventually revealed to all in the closing scenes.*

*Today, we call someone a **Tartuffe** if that person is a hypocrite of the highest order.*

---

tautology (noun)
= **expressing the same concept twice using different words (considered to be a fault of style)** from the Greek *tauto*: same, and *-logos*: word

e.g. The phrase 'frozen ice' is a tautology: all ice is frozen so there is no need for the adjective 'frozen'

tawdry (adj.)
= **sordid and unpleasant** *for etymology, see box below*

e.g. Many a glamour model has been paid a small fortune by the media to give a **tawdry** account of an affair with a married footballer

---

tawdry is a contraction of the name of Saint Audrey, an Anglo-Saxon saint.

*In the 17th century, devotees of Saint Audrey staged an annual fair where lace clothes would be sold. However, Puritans consider lace to look seedy and so it was that Saint Audrey – and the word **tawdry** that is a contraction of her name – became associated with tackiness.*

*Today, we use **tawdry** to describe something that is sordid and cheap.*

---

teleological (adj.)
= **relating to the explanation of living things by the purpose they serve rather than by their origins** from the Greek *telos-*: end, and *-logos*: word

e.g. Religious people believe that our lives are subject to a **teleological** framework

tendentious (adj.)
= **marked by a strong point of view, implicitly expressed**
from the Medieval Latin *tendentia*: a cause, from the Latin
tendere: to stretch

e.g. The BBC is required to produce programmes that
have no political or other agenda, so there is no
tendentious editing at the Beeb

tenebrous (adj.)
= **shadowy** from the Latin *tenebrae*: darkness

e.g. In his youth, Sean Connery worked as a coffin-
polisher in a **tenebrous** building occupied by a funeral
director

tenet (noun)
= **a principle** from the Latin *tenet*, which means 'he holds',
from the verb *tenere*: to hold

e.g. That Muhammad received a series of revelations
from God is one of the main **tenets** of Islam

termagant (noun)
= **a scolding woman** *for etymology, see box below*

e.g. Katherine Hepburn would insist on sniffing the hair of her co-stars to make sure it was clean: such intrusive behaviour is typical of a **termagant**

---

termagant was the name of a character in medieval morality plays.

*Termagant was a fictitious male Muslim deity with a violent nature who appeared in medieval morality plays. As **Termagant** wore long gowns, English audiences mistakenly believed the character was female.*

*Today, when we call a woman a **termagant**, it means she has a scolding nature.*

---

theocrat (noun)
= **a leader who rules in the name of God** from the Greek *theos*: god, *kratos*: rule

e.g. Until Japan's defeat in World War II – when Emperor Hirohito was forced to deny that the Emperor of Japan was divine – Japan was ruled by **theocrats**

tinnitus (noun)
= **a ringing sound in the ears (often caused by a specific condition such as a head injury)** from the Latin *tinnire*: to ring, tinkle

e.g. After leaving a loud pop concert, people often have tinnitus in both ears

tithe (noun)
= **ten per cent of someone's income that is contributed to the Church** from the Middle English *tithe*, from the Anglo-Saxon *tien*: ten

e.g. Hundreds of years ago, most Christians paid the **tithe**; now very few do

topography (noun)
= **the way the physical features of an area are arranged** from the Greek *topographia*, from *topos*: place, and *graphe*: writing

e.g. The SAS troops needed to become familiar with every nook and cranny of Pakistan so they spent months studying the country's **topography**

totalitarian (noun)
= **a person advocating a dictatorship that requires total submission to the state** from the Latin *totus*: whole, entire

e.g. World leaders hope the openness displayed by China at events such as the Olympics is a sign that the government is relaxing its **totalitarian** stance

totemic (of)

totemic (of) (adj.)
= **markedly symbolic (of)** *for etymology, see box opposite*

e.g. For most people the Queen is the **totemic** member of the Royal Family

totemic finds its root in the French word **aoutem***, which means an object considered by Indians to be the emblem of a clan.*

Totems were usually an animal or an object from nature; as well as being representative of a clan, totems were believed to protect the clansmen.

Today, when we describe a person or thing being as **totemic***, we mean that it is distinctly symbolic of something.*

touchstone (noun)
= **a benchmark by which something is judged** *for etymology, see box below*

e.g. Roger Federer holds more Grand Slam titles than any other player in the history of tennis; his achievement is the **touchstone** for all future players

A **touchstone** *refers to a piece of dark jasper which was used to test the purity of a gold alloy by observing the colour of the mark the alloys made on it.*

The streak left behind was compared to the clear yellow streak left by pure gold.

Today, we call something a **touchstone** *when it provides a standard by which to judge other things.
(See also* **paragon***, which has a near-identical meaning.)*

transmogrify (verb)
= **to transform, especially in a way that is not expected**
deriving from the verb *transmigrate*: (*of the soul*) to pass
into another body after death

e.g. When he invented Facebook, Marc Zuckerberg was
transmogrified from Harvard postgraduate to the
youngest self-made billionaire on the planet

trenchant (adj.)
= (*of language or a person*) **incisive and cutting** from the
Old French *trenchant*: cutting, from the verb *trenchier*, itself
based on the Latin, *truncare*: to maim

e.g. When people talk about failed romantic
relationships, their tone of voice often becomes
trenchant

triumvirate / troika (noun)
= **a group of three people working alongside each other**
triumvirate derives from the Latin trium virum, *the genitive
plural of* tres viri: *three men;* **troika** *derives from the Russian*
troe: *set of three*

e.g. A **triumvirate / troika** of film moguls – Spielberg,
Geffen and Katzenberg – set up the studio *DreamWorks*

trope (noun)
= **a common theme; OR the use of words in a non-literal
way, such as a metaphor** from the Greek *tropos*: turn, way

e.g. Much of the tension in the horror film *The Shining*
derives from the **trope** of the psychic child who has the
ability to foresee imminent evil

truculent (adj.)
= **quick to fight** from the Latin *trux, trucis*: fierce

e.g. Actor Errol Flynn blew the money he had saved for an engagement ring at the bookies; his **truculent** fiancée broke up with him as a result

turpitude (noun)
= **corruption** from the Latin *turpis*: disgraceful

e.g. The US government still bars from entering the country those people considered to be in a state of moral **turpitude**

tussock (noun)
= **a small patch of grass that is longer than the grass surrounding it** *tussock derives from a 16th-century alternation of 'tusk', which meant a 'tuft'*

e.g. If you have mowed your lawn properly no **tussocks** will remain

U

ululate (verb)
= **to utter howling sounds** from the Latin *ululare*: to howl, shriek

e.g. During the funeral scenes in the *Godfather* films, old women in black **ululate** around the coffin

utilitarian (adj.)
= **useful, rather than beautiful** from the Latin *utilis*: useful

e.g. Although most fridges are not beautiful, they are **utilitarian**

utopia (noun)
= **an imagined place in which everything is in perfect harmony** *for etymology, see box below*

e.g. Kristin Scott Thomas's father was a Royal Navy pilot; when he died in a flying accident, this shattered the **utopia** of her childhood

---

utopia has a rather depressing etymology – for it derives from the Greek words ou *(meaning 'not') and* topos *(meaning 'a place'): in other words, a* **utopia** *or a sense of happiness is a place that does not exist.*

The word **utopia** *was popularised by Sir Thomas More (who was beheaded by Henry VIII). In* Of the Best State of a Republic and of the New Island Utopia *(1516), More depicts the island of Utopia as a landmass where harmony reigns thanks to its perfect social and political structure.*

Today, we continue to refer to any perfect place as being a **utopia**.

(For the opposite of a **utopia** *– i.e. a place where discord reigns – see* **dystopia**.)

209

uxorious (adj.)
= *(of a husband)* **displaying an indulgent fondness for one's wife** from the Latin *uxor*: wife

e.g. On the TV show *Richard and Judy*, Richard's constant attention to his wife Judy gave the impression of an **uxorious** man

V

vagabond (noun)
= **a person without a home who wanders around** from the Latin *vagari*: to wander

e.g. After his widowed mother was certified insane, Charlie Chaplin left school to join a dance troupe and become, in effect, a **vagabond**

vagaries (pl. noun)
= **unforeseen changes in a situation** from the Latin *vagari*: to wander

e.g. Winston Churchill often felt the urge to throw himself off railway platforms because he was prone to the **vagaries** of manic depression

vainglorious (adj.)
= **characterised by vanity and boasting** from the Old French *vaine gloire*: vain glory

e.g. Some religious people regard atheists as being **vainglorious** for denying the existence of God

valedictory (adj.)
= **serving as a farewell** from the Latin *vale*: goodbye, and *dicere*: to say

e.g. In his final months in office, Tony Blair appeared on several TV chat shows in a kind of **valedictory** tour

vampish (adj.)
= **relating to a woman who uses sexual attraction to manipulate men** *vampish derives from an early 20th-century abbreviation of 'vampire'*

e.g. The nature of the relationship between John F. Kennedy and Marilyn Monroe was clear from the **vampish** way in which she sang: 'Happy Birthday, Mr President'

vapid (adj.)
= **dull, unstimulating** from the Latin *vapidus*: flat

e.g. The piped music played in aeroplanes awaiting take-off invariably is **vapid**

vaudeville (noun)
= **a stage play on a frivolous theme with songs along the way** *for etymology, see box below*

e.g. Musicals such as *Mary Poppins* owe a lot to the tradition of **vaudeville**, a theatrical genre of variety entertainment popular in the US until the 1930s

---

vaudeville derives from the French word vaudeville, *which in the 15th century meant 'a popular song'. (The word **vaudeville's** formation in France can be traced to the most famous writer of such songs who lived in the valley of Vire, or, in French, the* Vau de Vire*).*

*It was variety theatre owners in the US who adopted the expression **vaudeville** at the end of the 19th century in the hope that the Frenchness of the term might lend the halls an air of sophistication and thus differentiate them in the public's mind from the earlier variety halls which were marked by rowdiness.*

*Today **vaudeville** refers to any entertainment made up of a series of short musical sketches and with a light-hearted theme.*

(much) vaunted (phrase)
= **much praised** from the Old French *vanter*: to praise, based on the Latin *vanitare*: to talk frivolously (from the Latin *vanare*: to utter empty words, from *vanus*: empty)

e.g. When Charlie Chaplin came third in a Charlie Chaplin lookalike contest, he had to admit that the winner, a **much vaunted** lookalike, did indeed bear an uncanny resemblance to him

venal (adj.)
= **being open to bribery** from the Latin *venum*: thing for sale

e.g. One month before the invasion of Iraq, Saddam Hussein made an offer to stand down peacefully in return for $1bn; he remained **venal** to the last

venial (adj.)
= *(of a fault)* **trivial** from the Latin *venia*: forgiveness

e.g. Russian monarch Ivan the Terrible, who used to roast humans alive, regarded his other pastimes – such as throwing dogs off towers – as no more than **venial** sins

verbiage (noun)
= **writing that uses an excessive amount of words** from the French *verbe*: word

e.g. Walt Disney often spoke about the need for cleanliness; proving his words were no mere **verbiage**, he would wash his own hands up to 30 times an hour

verdant (adj.)

= *(of countryside)* **green with grass or other organic matter** from the Old French *verdoyant*: becoming green, based on the Latin, *viridare*: to grow green

e.g. A team of gardeners ensure the lawns of Buckingham Palace remain **verdant** at all times

vernacular (adj.)

= **the everyday language spoken by the people in one region** from the Latin *vernaculus*: native, from *verna*: home-born slave

e.g. Anti-Muslim attitudes are commonplace; this is reflected by the fact that the word 'Islamophobia' has entered the English **vernacular**

vicarious (adj.)

= **feelings experienced in one person's mind via someone else's descriptions or display of their own feelings** *for etymology, see box opposite*

e.g. When Fred Astaire's dancing prevented him from watching his beloved soap operas, he would phone his housemaid to experience the plot twists **vicariously**

vicarious

vicarious originates from the word 'vicar': both words are derived from the Latin *vicarius*, meaning 'substitute'.

In the Catholic Church, a vicar is the 'representative' of a bishop; similarly, when a friend tells us a story about his recent car crash, our friend becomes our 'representative' during the moments that the vehicle crumpled, and we experience the crash **vicariously***.*

vicissitude (noun)
= **a unpleasant change in a situation** from the Latin *vicissim*: by turns

e.g. When his wife died in a plane crash, Clark Gable kept her bedroom exactly as it was the day she caught the plane because he was so upset at this **vicissitude**

vilify (verb)
= **to talk about (someone) in a denigrating manner** from the Latin *vilis*: of low value

e.g. When Roger Clinton, half-brother of Bill, pleaded guilty to cocaine distribution, the press **vilified** him

visceral (adj.)
= **perceived as if in the internal organs (the viscera)** from the Latin *viscera*: the internal organs

e.g. To fall in love at first sight is to experience an immediate visceral response to someone

vista (noun)
= **a distant view especially one seen through an opening** from the Italian *visto*: seen, past participle of *vedere*: to see (from the Latin *videre*: to see); *a vista literally means: 'a pleasing view seen through a long, narrow opening'*

e.g. Dying of cancer in Switzerland, Audrey Hepburn had her bed positioned so she could see the mountains outside her window; she loved this **vista**

vitiate (verb)
= **to harm the quality of** from the Latin *vitiare*: to impair

e.g. Told he was too sane for a psychiatric hospital, Spike Milligan stabbed Peter Sellers; in this way he **vitiated** his record of sanity and was admitted

vituperate (verb)
= **to speak very disparagingly about someone** from the Latin *vituperare*: to disparage

e.g. When the 54-year-old Charlie Chaplin married the 18-year-old Oona O'Neill, the press **vituperated** him

voluptuary (noun)
= **a person devoted to self-indulgence** from the Latin *voluptas*: pleasure

e.g. As a **voluptuary**, Oscar Wilde loved sensual indulgence, especially an activity he called 'feasting with panthers', which meant going with rent boys

vulpine (adj.)
= **like a fox** from the Latin *vulpes*: a fox

e.g. Alsatians are the most **vulpine** of dogs

wainscot (noun)
= **an area of wooden panelling running along the bottom of some walls** from the medieval Flemish *waghenscote*: superior quality oak wood

e.g. Rooms in Victorian houses often have **wainscot** on the lower part of the walls of rooms

wanderlust (noun)
= **a yearning to travel** from the German *wandern*: to wander, and *lust*: lust

e.g. Graham Greene wrote novels set on several continents, all of which he had travelled across to sate his **wanderlust**

wanton (adj.)
= *(especially of a woman)* **sexually indecent; OR** *(of an action)* **deliberate and out of the blue** from the Middle English *wan-*: wanting, lacking, and *togen*: to discipline: *together these words imply a notion of 'badly disciplined/ badly brought up'*

e.g. When he was just 18, William Shakespeare married a woman who was already clearly pregnant, leading to gossip accusing her of **wanton** behaviour

waspish (adj.)
= **very irritable** from the word *wasp*, an insect renowned for its irritability

e.g. When working as a librarian, the poet Philip Larkin would ask people in a **waspish** tone: 'Why on earth are you borrowing drivel like that?'

wend (verb)

= **to travel slowly towards a particular goal** from the German *wenden*: to turn

e.g. When exploring a new city, tourists are in no rush usually preferring to **wend** their way around

wheedle (verb)

= **to convince someone using flattery** from the German *wedeln*: 'to wag the tail like a fawning dog', hence 'to fawn, flatter'

e.g. In 'honey-trap' operations, female police officers use their wiles to **wheedle** information out of male murder suspects

widow's peak (noun)

= **a V-shaped growth of hair in the centre of the forehead left behind as the hairline recedes** *for etymology, see box below*

e.g. With age, men often develop a **widow's peak**

---

widow's peak derives from the old wives' tale that a V-shaped hair pattern on a man's forehead means he will die soon, leaving his wife a widow.

winnow (down) (verb)
= **to reduce the number (in a collection of things) until only the best ones remain** from the Old English *windwian*: to ventilate, from *wind*: wind; *the literal meaning of **winnow** is 'to blow a current of air through (grain) in order to remove the chaff'*

e.g. Every year 128 tennis players compete in the men's singles at Wimbledon; by the day of the finals their number has been **winnowed down** to just two contestants

Sources

Cawthorne, Nigel. *Sex Lives of Hollywood Idols*. London: Prion Books, 2004.

Dillon-Malone, Aubrey. *Funny Peculiar: A Directory of the Daft and Dotty*. London: Prion Books, 2001.

Parish, James Robert. *The Hollywood Book of Death*. New York: McGraw-Hill, 2001.

Schnakenberg, Robert. *Secret Lives of Great Authors*. Philadelphia: Quirk Books, 2008.

Soanes, Catherine and Angus Stevenson. *Oxford Dictionary of English*. Oxford: Oxford University Press, 2005

Online Etymology Dictionary: www.etymonline.com

Acknowledgements

My debt is to the following:

my friend and agent Sheila Ableman who maintained a notebook of interesting words in her teenage years; Lisa Carden and Ellen Grace at A&C Black for their perspicacity; Sandra Howgate and the sense of the surreal in her drawings; my four brothers and six sisters and their gallows humour which sustains me; Kelly and her smile; Dom and his knowing when to work hard and when not to; Alex who blazed the trail; Louisa who likes to take apart clichés; Feras who gave me the word 'liminal'; David for swivelling his chair once in a while to activate the movement-sensitive light switch; Colin for his love of words and the quote he gave me; Charlie and his insistence on etymology; Piers for valuing writing; Michael for devoting three evenings to check over the script; Nigel for his help on all matters Classical; Rosemary for her inspiring idiosyncracy; Amanda and her understanding; and Harry whose exuberance produced the title.

Any reader can contact me here with criticisms, new words or anything else: hubert_vandenbergh@yahoo.co.uk